# COLLINS GEM

# GAMES FOR ONE

The Diagram Group

D1390546

HarperCollins*Publishers*

HarperCollins Publishers
P.O. Box, Glasgow G4 0NB

A Diagram Book first created by Diagram Visual
Information Limited of 195 Kentish Town Road,
London NW5 8SY, England

First published 1992
© Diagram Visual Information Limited 1992
Reprint 10 9 8 7 6 5 4 3 2 1 0

ISBN 0 00 470040 6

Printed in Great Britain by
HarperCollins Manufacturing, Glasgow

# Introduction

Most of us, at some time or other, find ourselves
alone, unoccupied and possibly even bored. Whether
waiting to see a doctor, for a train or needing to while
away a wet Saturday afternoon, we sometimes want
some form of amusement other than that provided by
television or a novel.

The *Collins Gem Games for One* fulfils this need: it is
a fascinating, detailed and highly illustrated directory
of scores of solitary pastimes, offering something to
everyone, young and old alike. From card games to
card tricks, from pangrams to tangrams and from cat's
cradle to magically disappearing knots in rope, *Collins
Gem Games for One* is a potpouri for the solo player.
Whether bedridden or airborne, you can learn how to
draw cartoons, make shadow figures, produce magic
squares and practise magic tricks with which to delight
your friends. With each game and activity, there are
step-by-step instructions and clear, accurate diagrams
showing techniques and methods that are easy to
follow.

Created by the Diagram Group, *Collins Gem Games
for One* is an attractive companion volume to the same
team's *Gem Family and Party Games* and *Gem Card
Games*.

# Contents

## 1. CARD GAMES

## 2. MAGIC TRICKS

## 6. WORD GAMES

## 7. NUMBER PUZZLES

## 8. PAPER GAMES

## 9. ACTION GAMES

# 1. Card games

## ACCORDION
A challenging game, it is also known as Methuselah or Tower of Babel.

### Cards
One standard 52-card deck is shuffled thoroughly.

### The layout
There is no formal layout. A single row of face-up cards is dealt out, as many as space permits. Surplus cards are put aside and dealt as space opens up.

### A sample layout

### Aim
To build the deck into one pile.

### Playing
Any card can be moved onto the card on its left or onto the third card from its left, if it matches in rank or suit. Other cards in the row can be added to this pile as long as they match the top card; and piles of cards can be moved in similar fashion, according to the rank and suit of the top card. When space becomes available, other cards can be added to the row.

The game is resolved when a single pile has been made of all the cards. If further moves are impossible before this happens, all cards should be collected and shuffled for a new layout.

## BELEAGUERED CASTLE

Also known as Laying Siege or Sham Battle.

## Cards

A standard 52-card deck is needed.

### A sample layout

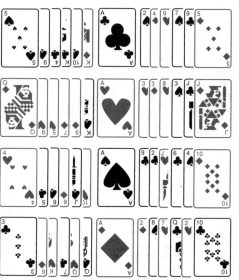

foundations

**The layout**

The four aces, known as the foundation cards, are placed face up in any order in a column. On the left of each ace, deal one card, face up. Then deal the same way to the right of each ace. Deal one card overlapping each of these, and continue dealing in this way, overlapping the cards as they are dealt, until there are 'arms' of six cards on each side of each ace.

**Aim**

To build on each foundation card a pile of each suit in numerical order from ace (low) up to K.

**Playing**

Any one of the eight exposed cards at the outer ends of the arms may be selected for play and placed either on the foundation pile of the same suit to build upwards, or on the end of any other arm to build numerically downwards. If an arm has no cards left, another end card can be played into the space.

**BISLEY**

Another game using foundation cards.

**Cards**

One standard deck of 52 cards is used.

**The layout**

First place the four aces in a row on the table, then increase the length of the row by nine cards dealt from the pack. Continue to deal the cards, making three more rows below the first one, until you have four rows, each of 13 cards.

**Aim**

To build suits in rank order, using the aces and the Ks as foundation cards.

## A sample layout for Bisley
foundations

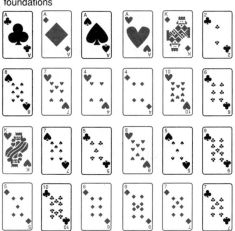

## Playing

Any of the bottom row of cards can be used to build on an ace of the same suit, numerically upwards, or to build onto another bottom-row card of the same suit, either upwards or downwards (the order of building may be reversed when desired or required).

When a K becomes available, it is placed in a new row above the ace of the same suit and can then be built on numerically downwards. When the two sequences of

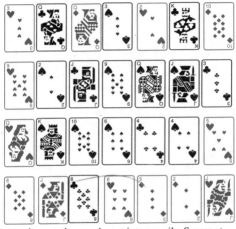

one suit meet, they can be put into one pile. Spaces at the bottom of columns are not filled, thereby making the cards above them available for play.

## BRAID

Also known as Plait, the game has a layout that takes the form of a braid or plait.

### Cards

Two standard decks of 52 cards are needed.

**The layout**

Twenty cards are dealt left and right diagonally, face up, overlapping as in a braid. Six cards are dealt face up in two columns either side of the braid. These columns are the reserve.

The next card is placed face up to one side of the reserve columns as the first foundation card; spaces are needed for seven more (which must be of the same rank as the first) and for a discard pile, as shown in the sample layout. The remaining stock of cards is retained for use.

**Aim**

To build two numerical sequences in each of the four suits, building upwards from the rank of the first foundation card and going "round the corner" from Q, K to ace, 2.

**Playing**

In the sample layout, the first foundation is 8D, so all the other seven foundation cards must be 8s.

Foundations may be built with reserve cards (in the

**A sample layout for Braid**

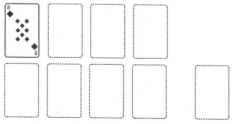

foundations                              discard pile

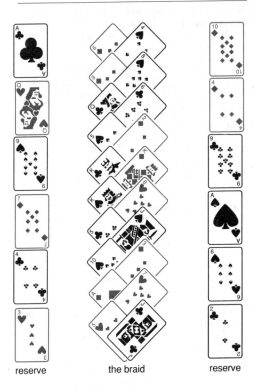

reserve      the braid      reserve

columns), with the exposed bottom card from the braid
or with cards from the stock.

Cards from the stock are played one at a time. If they
cannot be used to build they are placed face up on the
discard pile.

Spaces in the reserve columns must be filled
immediately. The stock is used to replace any of the
four middle cards. The top and bottom cards of a
column are replaced with either the exposed bottom
card from the braid or the top of the discard pile. The
cards can be redealt any number of times until the game
is played out or becomes blocked.

## BRISTOL

Aces are foundation cards in this game.

### Cards

One standard 52-card deck is used.

### The layout

Eight fans of three cards each are dealt face up. Ks are
placed at the bottom of the fans. Finally three cards are
dealt face up in a row to form three discard piles. The
stock is retained for play. Only one deal is allowed.

### Aim

To build four sequences in ascending numerical order
from ace, the foundation card, up to K, disregarding the
suits.

### Playing

Any top card from the discard piles or the fans can be
played, one at a time only.

The chosen card can be played in ascending numerical
order onto a foundation or in descending numerical
order onto the top card of a fan, disregarding suit.

Three cards are dealt face up from the stock, one to

each discard pile. This refills any spaces left by an
empty pile. When fans are used up, they are not
replaced.

**A sample layout**

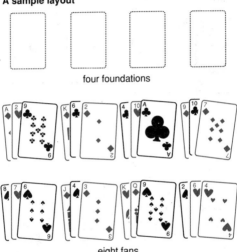

four foundations

eight fans

three
discard
piles

## CALCULATION
Also known as Broken Intervals, this game requires thought and foresight.

### Cards
One standard deck of 52 cards is needed.

**A sample layout**

four foundations

four discard piles

### A sample order of building

| on ace | on 2 | on 3 | on 4 |
|---|---|---|---|

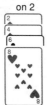

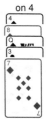

**The layout**

Choose any ace, 2, 3 and 4 and lay them in a row at the top of the table as foundation cards. All the remaining cards, held face down, are called the stock. Four discard piles are formed below the foundation cards as the game progresses.

**Aim**

Disregarding suit, the aim is to build on each foundation card in the following order:

On ACE, every card: ace, 2, 3, 4, 5, 6, 7, 8, 9, 10, J, Q, K.

On 2, every second card: 2, 4, 6, 8, 10, Q, ace, 3, 5, 7, 9, J, K.

On 3, every third card: 3, 6, 9, Q, 2, 5, 8, J, ace, 4, 7, 10, K.

On 4, every fourth card: 4, 8, Q, 3, 7, J, 2, 6, 10, ace, 5, 9, K.

**Playing**

One card at a time is turned up from the stock and may be placed overlapping any of the foundation cards, to begin building. If a card cannot be used to build, it may be placed face up on any of the four discard piles.

As the game continues, the top card of any discard pile may also be used to build, but may not be transferred to another discard pile.

The skill lies in controlling the cards in the discard piles. For example, Ks will be required last so it will be helpful to keep them either all in one pile or at the bottom of each pile.

Ideally, cards should be built on the discard piles in the order they will be needed to build on the foundations, i.e. in the reverse of the order shown above. Also, it is

advisable to scatter cards of the same rank throughout
the different discard piles.

In practice, many of the cards turned up from the stock
will enable the player to build on the foundation cards.
If a discard pile runs out, the space can be filled with a
new pile, if required. The maximum number of discard
piles at any one time is four.

## CANFIELD

Named in the USA after a 19th-century gambler and art
collector, this game is often known in the UK as Demon.

### Cards

One standard deck of 52 cards is used.

**A sample layout**

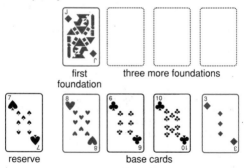

first
foundation

three more foundations

reserve

base cards

## The layout

First a pile of 13 cards (the reserve) is dealt face down,
then turned over leaving one card exposed.

The next four cards are placed face up in a row next to

the reserve; these form the base cards.

The next card is placed above the first base card and forms the first of a row of four foundations. Its rank determines the rank of all the foundation cards. If a base card already dealt matches the foundation card, it is moved up into the foundation row, and another is dealt in its place. The remaining cards form the stock.

## Aim

To build upwards, in suits, on the foundation cards, and to build downwards on the base cards, disregarding suit but in alternate colours, until all the cards are used from the stock, the reserve and the discard pile (if there is one).

## Playing

Three cards at a time are dealt from the stock, with only the top card exposed and available to be played. It may be played onto a foundation pile, a base pile or the discard pile. If it is the same rank as the first foundation card, it forms the next foundation.

Building on the foundations is done numerically upwards, in suits, K followed by ace, 2, etc.

Building on the base cards is done numerically downwards, in alternate colours of either suit. A sequence on a base card can be transferred to another base sequence, providing the colours still alternate and the sequence continues.

Cards from the reserve are used to fill spaces in the base. When the reserve is exhausted, the top card from the discard pile may be used to make a new base if required, or the base may be left empty.

When fewer than three cards remain in the stock, they are dealt one at a time.

**How the cards might be played in Canfield**

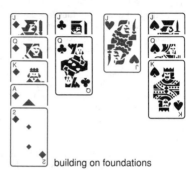

building on foundations

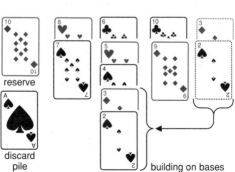

reserve

discard pile

building on bases

The whole layout may be redealt without shuffling, as often as desired, until the game either comes out or becomes blocked.

## CLOCK

This game has many names, such as Sundial, Travellers, Four of a Kind and Hidden Cards. It is a fast-moving, enjoyable game, but the chances of getting all the cards out are small.

### Cards

A standard deck of 52 cards is used.

### The layout

The cards are dealt face down, 12 piles of four making a clock face and the 13th pile of four cards in the centre. The cards may be dealt singly, dealing round the circle four times, or in groups of four at a time.

### Aim

To reorganise the cards so each pile is of the same rank and matches the position of the hours of the clock: aces at 1 o'clock, 2s at 2 o'clock and so on to Qs at 12 o'clock, leaving the Ks in the central pile.

### Playing

The top card of the central pile is turned up and placed under its appropriate position, for example an 8 would be placed under the 8 o'clock pile. The top card from that pile is then turned up and correctly placed, and so on.

If a card is turned up that belongs to the same pile, the procedure is the same.

The game can only be resolved if the last card to be turned up is the fourth K. If the fourth K is turned up before all the other piles are complete, the game would

**The layout for Clock**

be blocked. Therefore, when a K is turned up, an exchange is allowed. The K may be exchanged for any one face-down card on the table. This gives the player a slightly improved chance of winning the game, but the odds against the last card being the fourth K are still very high.

Consequently, players often repeat the game many times at great speed, hoping to win at least once!

# CONTENDING KNIGHTS

A simple game of chance in which the four Js win
points against each other.

## Cards

One standard deck of 52 cards is used.

## The layout

The four Js are laid out in a row in the following order:
heart, club, diamond, spade.

## Aim

To play three rounds, allotting even-numbered cards to
the red Js and odd ones to the black Js, and awarding
points to each J accordingly to determine a winner.

## Playing

Four cards are turned up from the stock and placed on
the table. If any are even numbered, regardless of suit
or sequence, they are placed in a pile near the J of
hearts, face up. Qs count as odd numbers, Ks as even.
More cards are turned up from the stock to replace any
used. Any odd-numbered cards are piled near the J of
clubs.

The process is continued for the J of diamonds and the
J of spades. Returning to the J of hearts again, play
continues until all the stock has been used up.

If a J cannot take any card in its turn, play passes to the
next J. If a J takes all four cards, because they are all
odd or all even, that J is given one card from each of
the other three Js, regardless of whether they are odd or
even.

When the stock is played out, a J whose pile has 12
cards or more scores one point for each card in excess
of 12.

The cards should be shuffled thoroughly before playing

**Playing on the layout for Contending Knights**

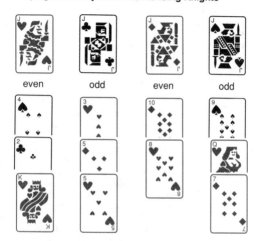

the next round. When three rounds have been played,
the winner is the J with the highest number of points.

**CRAZY QUILT**

A fascinating game requiring thought and skill, it is
also known as Japanese Rug or Indian Carpet. The
names reflect the interesting layout.

**Cards**

Two standard decks of 52 cards are needed.

**The layout**

Eight foundation cards are laid in a row by selecting an

ace and a K from each suit. In the space above the foundations, eight rows of eight cards each are dealt face up from the stock. Alternate cards are placed on their sides, forming a quilt pattern. These 64 cards are the reserve, and the remaining cards form the stock.

**Aim**

To build in suits, numerically upwards on the four ace foundations and numerically downwards on the four K foundations, until all 104 cards are in the eight foundation piles. The final piles can each be of any number.

**Playing**

Cards can be removed from the reserve onto the foundations providing one or both of their narrow edges is open. Thus, any of the 16 cards that project from the four sides of the quilt are immediately available. Removing one of these cards leaves two more available for play. Spaces in the reserve remain empty.

After available cards have been played from the reserve, one card is turned up from the stock and is used either to build or it is placed face up on the discard pile.

The top card on the discard pile is always available for play.

Providing there is already at least one card on the discard pile, available cards of the same suit from the reserve can be added to it in ascending or descending order. This rule can allow the release of a useful card from inside the quilt that does not have a narrow edge free.

If required, the stock can be shuffled and redealt once.

**A sample layout for Crazy Quilt**

reserve "quilt"

foundations

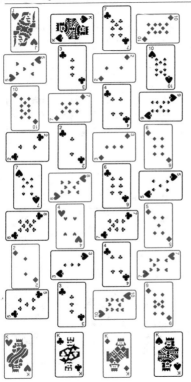

# EIGHT AWAY

This game features a layout of eight columns in which
there must never be more than eight cards. It is also
known as Eight Off.

## A sample layout

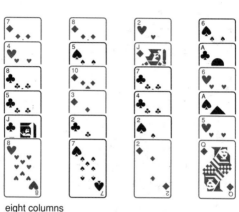

eight columns

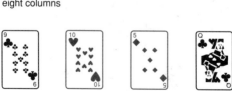

four reserves with space for up to four more

spaces for four foundations

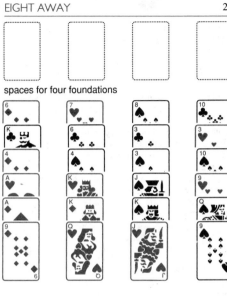

**Cards**

A standard deck of 52 cards is used.

**The layout**

Eight cards are dealt face up in a row. Five more rows of eight cards are dealt face up, each row overlapping the one above so that all cards can be seen.

The last four cards are turned face up in a row below the columns to form the reserve.

**Aim**

To move the aces above the layout to form four foundations and build on them numerically upwards to K in the same suit as each ace.

**Playing**

The exposed card at the bottom of each column and the four reserve cards are available for play. Cards can be used to build upwards on the foundations or downwards in suits on any other exposed card, or they can be moved to the reserve. Up to four more reserves can be made as needed. The reserve and the columns must each never contain more than eight cards. An empty column can only be replaced with an available K.

**FLORENTINE**

The layout of this game forms a five-card cross.

**Cards**

A standard deck of 52 cards is needed.

**The layout**

Five cards are turned face up and laid out to form a cross. The sixth card is placed, face up, at the top left corner of the table. This is the first foundation card, and its rank determines the rank of the other three foundations, which will be placed at the other three corners of the table as they come up during play.

**A sample layout for Florentine**

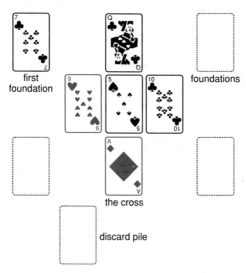

first foundation

the cross

foundations

discard pile

For example, if the first foundation is 7C, then the other three foundations will be 7D, 7S, 7H. If one of these cards comes up when forming the layout, or during play, it is immediately placed in a foundation position.

**Aim**

To build numerically upwards, in suits, on the four

foundation cards. The sequence from a Q, K would be
ace, 2, 3 and so on.

## Playing

One card at a time is played from the stock. It can be
used to build on the foundations. If it is not suitable its
suit is disregarded and it can be placed, in downwards
sequence, on any of the four outer "arms" of the cross.
If this is not possible, the card is placed face up on a
discard pile.

Cards may not be played onto the central card of the
cross.

When a card has been played from the stock, suitable
outer cards from the cross may be used to build on the
foundations, or on each other.

Spaces in the arms of the cross are filled by the central
card or a card from the discard pile. When the central
card is used, it is replaced by the top card from the
discard pile.

When the stock is exhausted, the discard pile can be
turned over, without shuffling, and used once as the
stock.

## FLOWER GARDEN

The layout for this game is called the flower garden,
individual fans of cards being the "flower beds" and
stock cards the "bouquet".

### Cards

One standard deck of 52 cards is used.

### The layout

Six fans of six cards each are dealt to form the flower
beds. The bouquet is the remaining stock, which may
be held in the hand or spread face up on the table. It
can be sorted into suits.

## A sample layout for Flower Garden

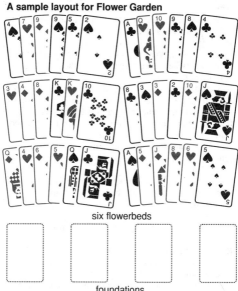

six flowerbeds

foundations

bouquet of 16 stock cards

**Aim**

To free the four aces and use them as foundations to
build upwards in suits, ace up to K.

**Playing**

In the sample layout, the two aces in the bouquet would
immediately be placed face up below the fans, starting
two of the foundations.

Any card from the bouquet or any exposed card from
the ends of the flower beds can be played. A card may
be used to build numerically upwards in suits on a
foundation ace, or to build downwards on the exposed
card of any flower bed, disregarding suit.

As long as the numerical order remains correct, a
sequence of cards may be moved from one flower bed
to another.

When a bed is used up, its space may be filled by one
card from the bouquet or a bed, or by a sequence from
another bed.

**FOURS**

A fast game using a piquet deck of 32 cards.

**Cards**

Remove all the 6s, 5s, 4s, 3s and 2s from a standard
deck. Shuffle the remaining 32 cards.

**The layout**

Deal four cards face up in a row. The stock should be
kept face down in the hand or on the table.

**Aim**

To make the cards come out in packets of four cards of
the same rank.

**Playing**

If two cards in the layout are of the same rank, place
them on top of each other, leaving a space in the row.

**Sample layout of a game of Fours in progress**

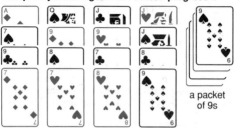

a packet of 9s

Turn up four cards from the stock, placing them in order in a row of four on top of (but not completely covering) the first cards and the space.

If any of these four cards in the new row are of equal rank, they are piled together on one of the columns and the spaces filled as the next row of four cards is turned up from the stock. The piles are not removed from the columns and row until there are four cards of equal rank, forming a "packet". In the sample game shown above, it is possible to create a packet of 9s by freeing them through moving and piling the cards that are on top of them, before the next row is dealt. Once a packet has been created, it is put aside and the next row is dealt, which will fill the space left by the packet.

**Packets**

These are collected in a pile, face up on top of each other. When the stock runs out, the pile of packets is turned face down and used as the stock, without shuffling. Play continues until all the packets have been made or the game is blocked.

## FRIDAY THE THIRTEENTH

A game built on 13 foundations, requiring careful choices during play.

### Cards

A standard deck of 52 cards is needed.

### The layout

Select any J, Q, K and ace and place them in a row in that order, left to right. These are the first four foundations. Space will be needed for another nine foundations, from 2 to 10. The remaining stock is kept face down.

### A sample layout

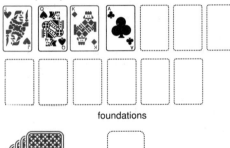

foundations

the stock

discard pile

**Aim**

To bring out nine more foundations while building piles of four cards upwards, in numerical order, on all 13 foundations, disregarding suit and colour.

**Playing**

Turn up one card at a time from the stock. It may be used to build on an existing foundation or to become a new foundation.

Foundations must be laid in correct rank order. A 2 must be laid down first, after which a 3 can be laid, and so on. If the option occurs, it is usually more helpful to put out a foundation card rather than to use it for building.

Building on foundations must be done numerically upwards, until there are four cards in each pile. For example, on the Q build any K, ace, 2; on the 8 build any 9, 10, J. Both suit and colour are disregarded in this game.

Cards may not be taken from one pile and used to build on another.

If a card cannot be used, it is placed face up on the discard pile. The exposed card on the discard pile is always available for play. If the stock runs out, the discard pile is turned face down and used as the stock. This is allowed only once.

**FROG**

Also known as Toad-in-the-hole, this game uses eight aces as foundations.

**Cards**

Two standard 52-card decks are used, making 104 cards.

## The layout

A reserve of 13 cards is dealt face up. Any aces among
these are laid out as foundations and cards are added to
the reserve to make up 13 cards. If an ace does not

**A sample layout for Frog**

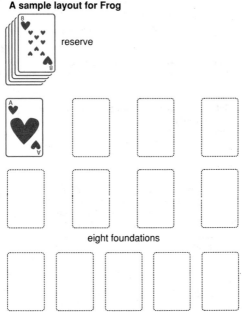

reserve

eight foundations

five discard piles

appear, one is found from the stock and placed in position. The remaining seven aces will be laid out as foundations as they appear during play. Space will also be required for five discard piles.

## Aim

To build numerically upwards, from 2 to K, on the eight foundations, disregarding suit and colour. The game is complete when the top card of each foundation pile is a K.

## Playing

One card at a time is turned up from the stock and added to a foundation or placed on one of the five discard piles.

## The discard piles

Cards can be added to any discard pile. The exposed card of each is always available for play.

It is useful to keep one pile for, say, high-value cards. Cards should be added to discard piles in reverse numerical order – for example, 10, 9, 8 rather than 8, 9, 10 – to avoid burying the lower-ranking cards that will be needed first. Spaces in the row of discard piles are filled from the stock.

## The reserve

The exposed card of the reserve is always available for play. When the reserve runs out, it is not replaced.

## GOLF

A great game for housebound golfers.

## Cards

A standard deck of 52 cards is used.

## The layout

Turn seven cards face up, placing them in a row to become the start of seven columns. Build the columns by placing another card face up below each one. Repeat until there are five cards in each of the seven columns, all clearly visible. This arrangement is called the links. The remaining 17 cards are placed face down in a pile and form the stock of golf clubs.

## Aim

To get the lowest possible score by using the stock of golf clubs to "clear" the links. For a nine-hole round, the game would be played nine times.

## Playing

Turn one card face up from the stock to form the hole. Any card from the links can then be played onto this card, regardless of suit, providing it follows in numerical sequence, upwards or downwards. Ace counts as low, so the top card of a sequence would be a K.

The direction can be reversed – for example, cards from the links might be available to build on a 3 in a downwards sequence, 2, ace, followed by an upwards sequence, 2, 3, 4, 5.

When it becomes impossible to play any more cards from the links, another card is turned up from the stock, placed on the hole and the process of building in sequence begins again.

When there is a choice about which way to build the sequence, it is helpful to remember which cards have already been played.

When the stock is exhausted, the number value of the cards remaining on the links is totalled. J, Q, K count as 10 each. The total is the score for the hole. If the links have been cleared and no cards remain in the stock, the score is 0. As in golf, the lower the score the better.

**A sample layout for Golf**

the links

the stock of
golf clubs

the hole

For a nine-hole game, the cards are shuffled and a new
layout is dealt eight more times.

# KING ALBERT
King Albert I of Belgium lent his name to this game.

## A sample layout

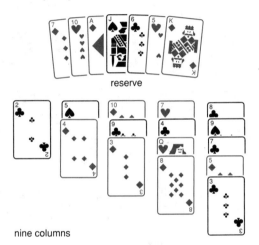

reserve

nine columns

## Cards

A standard deck of 52 cards is used.

## The layout

Nine cards are dealt face up in a row to form nine

foundations

columns. Cards are dealt onto the columns in rows, from left to right, so that there is one card in the first column, two cards in the second, three in the third and so on. There will be nine cards in the last column. Cards should overlap slightly and leave only the bottom card in each column fully exposed.

The last seven cards form the reserve and are spread face up in a fan. Space is also required for four foundations (the aces).

## Aim

To release the four aces during play and build upon them in suits in ascending order up to K.

## Playing

All cards in the reserve and the exposed bottom card in each column are available for play. One card at a time may be moved either onto the bottom of another column or onto a foundation pile once the aces have become available.

Building on the columns is by alternate colours in descending numerical order. Building on the foundations is by suit in ascending numerical order up to K.

A card from a foundation may be moved onto a column, provided it fits into the sequence correctly.

When a column has been used up, any card may be used to fill the space.

The game is complete when all cards have been built onto the foundations.

## KLONDIKE

An attractive, fast-moving game combining judgement and luck. It is sometimes known in the UK as Canfield, not to be confused with the American game of that name described earlier.

**A sample layout for Klondike**

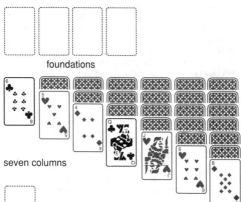

foundations

seven columns

discard
pile

## Cards

A standard deck of 52 cards is needed.

## The layout

Deal one card face up and six more face down in a row
from left to right. Along the next row, deal one card
face up on the second column and five more face down
on the remaining columns, partly overlapping the first
row.

Along the next row deal one card face up on the third
column and four more face down on the remaining four

columns.

Continue in this way until the last column has six face-down cards and one face-up card at the bottom.

The undealt cards are held face down in the hand and form the stock.

## Aim

To place the four aces as foundations when they become available during play and to build upon them in suits in ascending order up to K.

## Playing

Only one card is played at a time. It can be the top card from the stock or any of the exposed cards from the columns. Any card from the stock which cannot immediately be played is placed face up on a discard pile. The top card of this pile is available for play.

A card may be placed onto an exposed card in the columns, in alternate colours and descending numerical order. Once the foundation aces are released during play, cards may then be built onto them in suits in ascending numerical order.

As a card is removed from a column, the next card is turned face up. When a column is used up, its space may only be occupied by a K. The K may be from anywhere in the layout and brings with it any cards already built onto it.

Sequences may be transferred from one column to another as a complete unit.

## LA BELLE LUCIE

Cards are placed in fan shapes in this game, creating an attractive layout.

## Cards

A standard 52-card deck is needed.

## A sample layout for La Belle Lucie

foundations

17 fans and a single card

**The layout**

Deal all the cards face up into 17 fans of three cards each. The remaining card is dealt face up alone.

**Aim**

To release the four aces as foundations on which to build, in suits and in ascending numerical order, ace up to K.

**Playing**

The single card and the exposed card of each fan are available to be played. One card at a time is moved either to build onto a foundation, once the aces have been released, or to build numerically downwards on the top card of a fan in the same suit.

Building down onto a fan should be done with care as any cards underneath will be inaccessible. Spaces left by the complete removal of fans are not filled.

**Blocked game**

When the game becomes blocked because no more cards can be moved, all cards, except those already built onto foundations, are collected and shuffled. They are redealt into fans of three cards plus a pair or a single. Play then continues as before.

If the game becomes blocked again, one more deal takes place, as before. After this second redeal, the first card to be played may be any card on the table. No further redeal takes place.

# LEAPFROG

**Cards**

A standard 52-card deck is needed.

**The layout**

Deal four rows each with five separated face-up cards. The remaining stock is placed face down on the table.

## A sample layout for Leapfrog

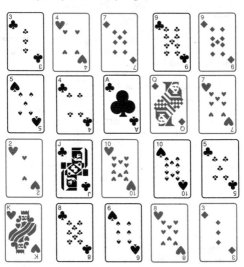

four rows of five

discard pile

**Aim**

To create as many unfilled spaces in the layout as possible, after using up the stock.

**Playing**

Any card in the layout may "leapfrog" over its neighbour in any direction horizontally, vertically or diagonally, as long as its destination is a card of the same rank or suit. The card that is leapt over is removed and placed face down on a discard pile. The two spaces created by a single leap are filled with face-up cards from the stock. A pile of two or more cards can also leapfrog according to the same rules; the top card of the pile is the identifying card. A card or a pile may also leapfrog several cards in succession, creating more spaces in one turn.

When the stock is exhausted, the aim is to make as many spaces as possible before the game is blocked.

**MAZE**

This game offers great satisfaction but requires time and skill.

**Cards**

A standard deck of 52 cards is needed.

**The layout**

All the cards are dealt face up: two rows of eight cards above, and four rows of nine cards below. The four Ks are removed, leaving six empty spaces on the table.

**Aim**

To rearrange the cards, one at a time, so that all cards are in suit sequences, ace to Q, from left to right. The suits can be in any order – for example, ace S to QS, followed by diamonds, hearts and clubs, each in sequence.

The cards may occupy any of the positions in the six rows, but rows may not be extended beyond their original length. A sequence may begin anywhere, each line following on from the end of the one above. The bottom line runs on to the beginning of the top line.

**Playing**

Any card can be moved into any of the spaces created by the discarded Ks, provided it makes a correct sequence with one of its new neighbours. For example,

6D can only be moved to a space with 5D on its left or
7D on its right.
If a space occurs to the right of a Q, it may be filled

**A sample layout for Maze with Ks removed**

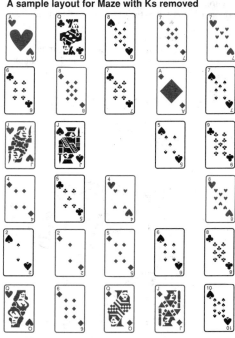

with any ace, even if there is not yet a neighbouring 2. Success can be achieved by thinking ahead before making a move.

## MISS MILLIGAN

An interesting game using eight foundations.

### Cards

Two standard decks are used, making 104 cards.

### Example of play

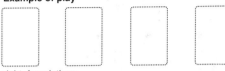

eight foundations

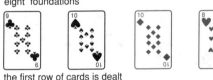

the first row of cards is dealt

ace moved onto foundation space

cards transferred and
ready for the second deal

**The layout**
Space will be needed for eight foundations. The game
begins by dealing a card face up below each foundation

space. This forms the first row of cards. The stock of cards is held face down in the hand.

## Aim

As the aces appear during play they are placed on the foundation spaces. The aim is then to build upwards on each ace in suit sequence.

## Playing

Any aces from the first row are moved onto the foundation spaces. Other cards from the first row can then be built either on an ace in ascending suit sequence or onto another first-row card in alternate colours in descending sequence – for example, black 10, red 9, black 8 and so on.

A second row of cards is then dealt overlapping the first row and filling empty spaces. Cards may then be moved onto foundation aces or onto other columns as before. Two or more cards can be moved together if they are in correct sequence.

Spaces made from this point onwards may only be filled by a K, together with any cards already built on it.

Cards continue to be dealt onto the columns and moved as before. It is best to make all possible transfers before making the next deal.

## Weaving

When the stock is used up, any single card, or sequence of cards, from one column may be lifted and used as a reserve. All the cards in the reserve then become available to build on foundations or other columns. This is known as weaving.

If all the cards in the reserve are used up to build, the weaving process can be repeated. However, if any card in the reserve cannot be used, the game is lost.

Weaving can be repeated until the aim of the game is achieved or the game becomes blocked.

## MONTE CARLO

Also known as Double and Quits or Weddings, this game requires players to make pairs.

### Cards

A standard deck of 52 cards is needed.

### The layout

Four rows of five cards are dealt face up. Players may prefer to play with five rows of five cards.

**A sample layout**

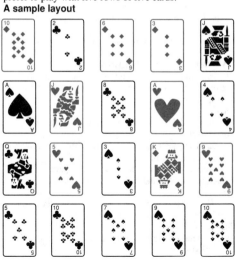

## Aim

To clear the table by pairing cards from the layout.

## Playing

Any two adjacent cards of the same rank are paired and removed from the layout. The pairing cards may be neighbours at the side, top, bottom or corners.

The spaces are filled by moving the layout cards in the same row to the left, and filling the end space(s) with cards from the row below. The cards should not be rearranged, only moved from right to left or upwards. After the cards are thus moved, the layout is rebuilt to its starting size with cards from the stock, and further pairing is done.

Play continues until all the cards are paired or until the game is blocked because no more cards can be paired.

# NAPOLEON AT ST HELENA

Also known as Big Forty and Forty Thieves, this is one of many patience games that may have been played by Napoleon.

## Cards

Two standard decks are used, totalling 104 cards.

## The layout

Ten cards are dealt face up in a row. Three more rows of ten cards are dealt, each overlapping the last, making ten columns of four overlapping cards. Space will be needed for eight foundations and a discard pile.

## Aim

To build upwards from ace to K, in suits, on the eight foundation spaces, playing all the cards.

## Playing

As aces become available they are placed on the foundation spaces.

The bottom card of each column is available and may be played either onto a foundation or onto another column, always building upwards in suits.

Alternatively, a card may be turned up from the stock
(which is used only once). If it cannot be used it is
placed face up on the discard pile, and remains
available for play until another card is put on top of it
(overlapping, so that the ones beneath are visible).

## A sample layout for Napoleon at St Helena

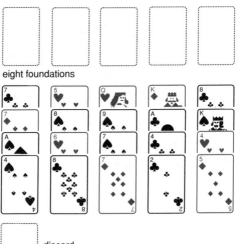

eight foundations

discard
pile

When a column disappears a new column is begun with
any available card. It is best to choose this card with
care, keeping in mind its usefulness for bringing others
into play.

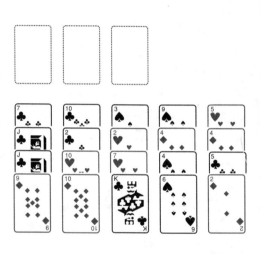

## POKER SOLITAIRE

A good way to learn how to play poker, this absorbing game requires good luck and good judgement.

### Cards

A standard 52-card deck is needed.

### The layout

Space will be needed for five rows of five cards, which will be dealt face up during play. Each row and each column is called a poker hand. There will be space for ten hands.

### Aim

To place cards anywhere in the rows and the columns to give the highest possible poker score, using either the British or the American scoring system.

### Playing

As the cards are turned up from the stock they may be placed anywhere on the layout – Ace can rank high or low but may not form a link – i.e., K, ace, 2 is not permitted.

### The nine hands

| Name | Combination |
| --- | --- |
| Royal flush | ace, K, Q, J, 10 of the same suit |
| Straight flush | 5-card sequence in same suit |
| Four of a kind | 4 cards of one rank + 1 odd |
| Full house | 3 same-rank cards + 2 of another rank |
| Flush | 5 cards of one suit |
| Straight | any 5-card sequence |
| Three of a kind | 3 same-rank cards + 2 odd |
| Two pairs | 2 pairs + 1 odd |
| One pair | 1 pair + 3 odd |

## The layout spaces

## The scoring systems

| Name of hand | American score | British score |
|---|---|---|
| Royal flush | 100 | 30 |
| Straight flush | 75 | 30 |
| Four of a kind | 50 | 16 |
| Full house | 25 | 10 |
| Flush | 20 | 5 |
| Straight | 15 | 12 |
| Three of a kind | 10 | 6 |
| Two pairs | 5 | 3 |
| One pair | 2 | 1 |
| None of the above | 0 | 0 |

An excellent score would be 200 (American) or 60 (British).

## Other rules

**1** The joker may be included in the deck and can represent any card. It may simply be added to the stock before dealing or may be used to replace a card after the deal has been played.

**2** The 25 cards can be dealt out in the order they are turned up and then can be rearranged to make the best hands.

**3** A more difficult variation is to limit the placing of each card to a position neighbouring the last one: side, top, bottom or corner.

## PUSS IN THE CORNER

This game derives its name from the fact that discard piles are placed at the corners of the square foundation layout.

### Cards

One standard deck of 52 cards is needed.

### The layout

The four aces form the foundations and are placed face up in a square. Leave space around them for the discard piles.

### Aim

To build numerically upwards on each foundation, from ace to K, in the same colour but disregarding suit.

### The layout for Puss in the Corner

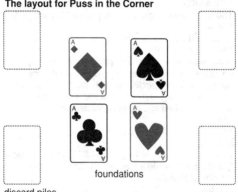

foundations

discard piles

### Playing

Cards are turned up from the stock one at a time and played onto a foundation, if possible, or thrown face up onto any discard pile.

It is best to keep one discard pile for the high-ranking court cards and to avoid putting high-ranking cards on top of those of low rank.

The top card on each discard pile is always available for play.

If the stock runs out before the game is resolved, one redeal is allowed. The four discard piles are gathered up in any order and used as the stock without shuffling. It is helpful to remember which cards are in which discard pile when collecting them.

## PYRAMID

This game seems easy, but luck plays a big part.

### Cards

A standard 52-card deck is needed.

### The layout

A pyramid shape is made by placing cards face up in seven rows, each row one card wider than the one before. Cards overlap leaving only the bottom row of seven cards completely exposed and available at the start of play. Two discard piles are needed.

### Aim

To make pairs, using all 52 cards.

Ignoring colour and suit, cards make pairs if their values total 13. Ace is 1, Q 12 and J 11, so an ace and a Q make a pair; so do a J and a 2. Ks are worth 13 and are played alone.

### Playing

Play begins by turning up a card from the stock and either pairing it up with an available card from the pyramid or placing it on either discard pile.

Pairs may be made from:

**1** the stock card and a pyramid card;

**2** two available pyramid cards; or

**3** the stock card and the top card of either discard pile.

If the stock pile is exhausted before all cards have been

paired, there may be one redeal by collecting both discard piles and using them as the stock pile.

## A sample layout for Pyramid

the pyramid

discard piles

## ROYAL COTILLION

This game takes its name from an 18th-century dance
that was performed at the French court.

### Cards

Two standard decks are used, making 104 cards.

### The layout

Find an ace and a 2 of each suit and place them
centrally in two columns, aces on the left. These eight
cards are the foundations. Some players prefer to lay

**A sample layout**

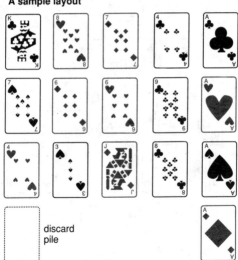

discard
pile

down the aces and 2s as they become available during play.

Twelve cards are dealt face up, in three rows of four cards, to the left of the top three aces; and 16 cards, in four rows of four cards, are dealt to the right of the 2s.

**Aim**

To build in suits on the foundations:

on aces: 3, 5, 7, 9, J, K, 2, 4, 6, 8, 10, Q

on 2s: 4, 6, 8, 10, Q, ace, 3, 5, 7, 9, J, K

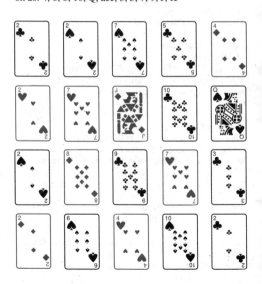

## Playing

The bottom card of each column in the left-hand group is available for play. Spaces created are not filled in this group. All cards in the right-hand group are available for play and spaces must be filled immediately with the top card of the stock or of the discard pile.

Cards are turned up one by one from the stock. If a card cannot be used to build, it is placed face up on the discard pile.

The top card of the discard pile is always available for play.

No redeal is allowed.

## SCORPION

This game does have a sting in its tail because if the hidden cards are not revealed early, they can block further moves towards the end of the game.

### Cards

A standard 52-card deck is needed.

### The layout

Deal a row of seven cards, the first four face down and the last three face up. Deal two more rows in the same way, each overlapping the previous row. Finally deal four more rows of cards all face up.

The three remaining cards are the reserve and are placed face down below the rows.

The four Ks will be the foundation cards. They are not removed from the layout.

### Aim

To build on the Ks in suits in descending order, down to the aces.

**Playing**

Building can only take place on fully exposed cards –
i.e., the bottom card in each column. Any appropriate
card in the layout can be used to build and takes with it
cards below it in the column. For example, if 4H is
exposed, 3H can be built onto it together with all its
overlapping cards, as shown overleaf. This move also
leaves a Q available for building.

Aces cannot be built on.

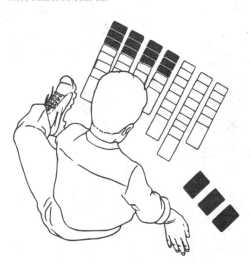

**The layout for Scorpion**

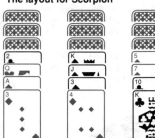

49 cards in seven columns

reserve

**Example of play**

3H is built onto 4H

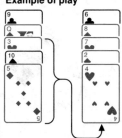

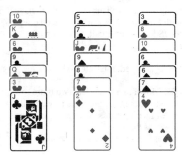

### Face-down cards

If a face-down card is exposed, it can then be turned over and is available for play. It is best to try and release the face-down cards early in the game to improve the chances of completing all the building.

### Spaces

When a column has been cleared, the space may be filled by a K, plus all the cards below it. Spaces do not have to be filled immediately.

### The reserve

Reserve cards are turned up only when no further moves are possible. They can only be added to the bottom of the three left-hand columns. Provided no other moves are possible, the reserve can be turned up before any column spaces are filled, giving the player greater choice.

## SPIDER

A game with many variations. This one is said to have been popular with Franklin D. Roosevelt when he was president of the USA, and some call it the king of patience games.

**Cards**

Two standard decks are used, totalling 104 cards.

**The layout**

Deal ten cards face down in a row. Deal two more rows face down, each overlapping the previous row. Finally deal a fourth row of face-up cards. The remaining cards are kept, face down, as the stock.

The eight Ks are the foundation cards and remain in the layout.

**Aim**

To build on the Ks in suits in descending order down to

**A sample layout**

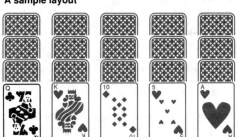

ace and discard each completed sequence until the table
is cleared.

**Playing**

All ten cards at the foot of the columns are available
for play. Any of these cards may be built onto another
in descending rank order, regardless of suit or colour. A
card that is used to build takes with it any others below
it. Nothing can be built onto an ace.

When a face-down card is exposed, it is turned face up
and is available for play.

Any spaces may be filled by any available card or by a
K with any cards below it.

**The stock**

When no more moves are possible, ten more cards are
dealt face up from the stock onto the foot of each
column. Play continues as before. The final deal of four
cards is onto the four left-hand columns.

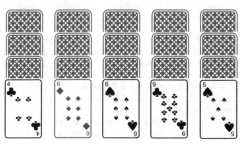

## WINDMILL

Sometimes known as Propeller, this game has a layout resembling either propeller blades or the sails of a windmill.

### Cards

Two standard decks are needed, totalling 104 cards.

### The layout

Any K is placed face up in the centre. A reserve of eight cards is built face up, two on each side of the king, to represent the sails. Space for four foundations will be needed and a discard pile.

### Aim

There are two aims:

**1** to build on the central K, in descending order, regardless of colour or suit. The sequence should consist of 13 cards from K to ace repeated four times to make a total sequence of 52 cards; and

**2** to build on the first four aces that become available in ascending order, regardless of suit or colour.

### Playing

One card at a time is turned up from the stock and is used either to build or is placed on the discard pile. The first four aces are placed in the foundation spaces in the corners of the "sails".

Cards from the stock, the sails and the top of the discard pile are all available for play onto the four ace foundations and the central K.

In addition, cards from the top of the ace piles can be used to build on the central K. Building on the K helps to resolve the game.

**A sample layout with central K**

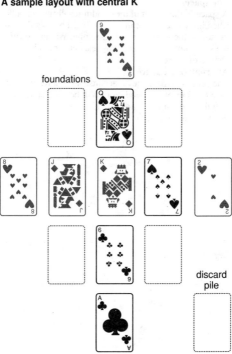

foundations

discard
pile

**The spaces**

A space in the layout of the windmill sails need not be
filled immediately. It can only be filled by a card from
the top of the stock or the discard pile. Waiting to fill
the space until a useful card appears enhances the
chance of success.

**Alternative sequences**

The central card can be an ace instead of a K, in which
case the four other foundations will be Ks. Sequences
will then be built upwards on the central ace and
downwards on the four Ks.

# GLOSSARY

**available** A card is called available when it fulfils the rules for use in play.

**blocked** A game that cannot possibly be won.

**building** Piling cards on top of each other during play in the order prescribed by the particular game. Most often by suit or by colour in numerical order, upwards or downwards.

**coming out** A game that achieves its aim and is totally resolved.

**dealing** Laying out the cards before play begins.

**deck** Pack or set of playing cards used for a game. Patience games are sometimes played with cards a size smaller than usual if space is at a premium.

**discard** Cards thrown away during play, usually into a discard pile.

**discard pile** Cards are thrown face up on this pile when they cannot be immediately used to build. They can be brought back into play later, as appropriate.

**exposed card** Normally only face up, completely exposed cards are available for play. Cards partly covered are unavailable until fully exposed.

**follow suit** Building with a card of the same suit as the previous one on the pile.

**foundations** Cards on which building takes place.

**layout** The arrangement in which the cards are dealt onto the table ready for play.

**packet** A given number of cards conforming to a particular requirement – e.g., a packet may be four cards of the same rank.

**patience** General name of card games for one player.

**piquet deck** A deck of 32 cards formed by removing all cards below the 7s from a standard 52-card deck, leaving 7, 8, 9, 10, J, Q, K, ace of each suit.

**rank** Order of cards, or suits, in play. Higher ranks take precedence over lower ranks.

**reserve** Cards in the layout that are available for play but are not foundations.

**round the corner** The order of cards when joining the ends of a sequence – e.g., Q, K, ace, 2, 3.

**solitaire** Sometimes synonymous with patience but also the name of a board game in its own right.

**spaces** Gaps in the layout that may or may not be filled, according to the rules of the game.

**stock** Cards remaining face down in the hand when dealing is complete. They are used in play according to the rules of each game.

**suit** Clubs, spades, hearts or diamonds.

# 2. Magic tricks

Being able to perform tricks that amaze and puzzle friends is a delight. To do this successfully, it is important to spend time alone practising until tricks can be performed easily and in a relaxed manner.

The name "conjuror" was given to someone who, it was once believed, called upon supernatural forces to perform "magic" tricks. Nowadays, a conjuror is understood to be a person who has learnt how to do tricks.

## TYPES OF MAGIC TRICK

Some tricks require special equipment; others can be done with simple props, such as coins, string or matches.

**Illusions** are carried out by experienced magicians using large, expensive pieces of equipment to make people, things or animals seemingly vanish, levitate or be cut in half!

**Escapology** (escaping from ropes, chains, boxes, etc.) can be dangerous. While some trickery is used, much escapology depends on speed, fitness, agility and skills, such as lock-picking.

**Mentalism** depends on creating the illusion of supernatural powers of the mind by apparently predicting future events, reading thoughts and making irrational things happen, such as bending forks.

**Prestidigitation** comes from the old French word *preste*, meaning nimble, and the Latin *digitus*, meaning finger. A prestidigitator is a person who performs magic tricks using hand manipulation, or sleight of hand. (The French word *legerdemain* also means sleight of hand.)

The tricks presented here for practice are of this last type.

Good prestidigitators practise four kinds of skilful manipulation:

**1** to produce things as if by magic;

**2** to repair breakages as if by magic;

**3** to transport things magically from place to place;

**4** to "vanish" things, a term used by magicians when they seemingly make things disappear.

**Types of magic trick**

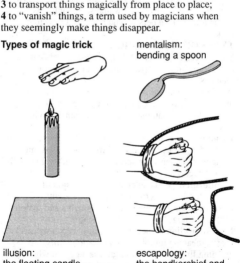

mentalism:
bending a spoon

illusion:
the floating candle

escapology:
the handkerchief and
rope trick

prestidigitation:
the vanishing coin trick

## SLICED BANANA

This trick produces a ready-sliced banana. Is it a new
variety? No, just a carefully prepared magic trick that
will amaze anyone who happens to pick the banana
from the fruit bowl and peel it.

### Equipment

You will need one large, yellow banana; a long, sharp
needle, such as is used for darning; and some fine,
strong polyester or nylon thread.

### The trick

Thread the needle, pulling it through to double it. Then
clean both the needle and thread by immersing them for
a few seconds in boiling water.

**1** Push the threaded needle through the banana skin, but
not into the flesh, and out again at a point further round
the circumference of the banana.

**2** Push the needle back in through the last hole and out
again further round.

**3** Continue "sewing" until you can bring the needle out
through the first hole. It may take four stitches to get
round the banana.

**4** When the stitching is complete, pull both double ends
of thread, cutting through the flesh, leaving the peel
unbroken.

The banana has now been sliced at one point within its
peel. Repeat several times at different points on the banana.

**5** To check that the trick works, peel the banana. It
will fall into neat slices if the sewing has been done
correctly.

Leave a completed banana in the fruit bowl and watch
the surprise on someone's face when they peel it to find
a ready-sliced banana!

### Cross-section through a banana showing sewing technique

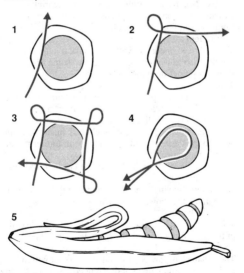

# TRICKS WITH COINS

Coin magic depends on manual dexterity and the ability
to hide coins in the hands, a skill known as "palming".
With a little practice, palming can be learnt using
ordinary coins such as ten-pence pieces, or coins of
similar weight and size.

## Palming a coin

Success comes from keeping the hands relaxed and
moving easily, rather than from gripping the coin
tightly. Six types of palming are shown here.

A good way to practise each one is by trying to palm a
coin while doing something else with your hands, such
as using the telephone, writing, drinking from a cup or
using hand gestures in casual conversation. Don't
practise while doing anything that needs your full
attention, such as pouring boiling water!

## 1 Standard palming

The coin is placed in the centre of the palm and gripped
lightly between the fleshy parts at the base of the thumb
and the outer side of the hand.

## 2 Thumb clipping

The edge of the coin is held between the thumb and the
hand. This method does not allow the free use of the
thumb but is useful for many coin tricks.

## 3 Finger clipping

The edge of the coin is held between two fingers.

## 4 Finger resting

The hand is held in its natural curled position with the
coin resting on the fingers.

## 5 Finger holding

The coin is gripped by the lower joints of the middle
(second) and ring (third) fingers.

### 6 Back palming

The coin is held in place, at the back of the hand, by its edge being gripped between the middle and ring fingers.

### Palming a coin

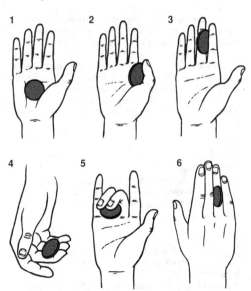

### The vanishing coin trick

This is a trick of "misdirection", the term used by magicians when the attention of an audience is held in one direction while the trick takes place elsewhere. In this case, attention is directed to the left hand while the right hand hides a coin.

### The illusion

A coin held in the right hand (**1**) is slapped down onto the left hand (**2**) three times. Each time, the right hand is raised to show the coin in the left hand before the coin is picked up in the right hand and slapped down again. The third time, the coin is not in the left hand and has apparently disappeared (**3**).

### The vanishing coin trick

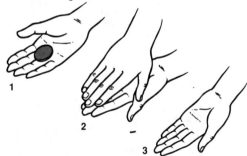

### How to practise the trick

Every time the right hand is raised, it should be bent back over the shoulder, while keeping your full attention on the left hand. A slightly bent neck helps.

When the right hand is raised for the third time, let the coin slip down between your neck and shirt collar, and immediately slap the hand down again. (Make sure your shirt is tucked in at the waist of your skirt or trousers – or else the coin will fall to the floor, alerting the audience to your trickery.)

Because the audience has seen the coin slapped down twice, they will keep watching the left hand and not notice what the right hand is doing.

Suggestions that the coin was thrown away or slipped up a sleeve can easily be disproved.

### How to practise the trick

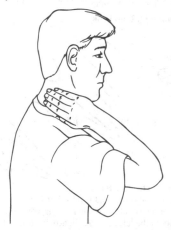

### The double-headed coin trick

When the right hand, holding a coin heads up, is turned over and slapped down onto the left hand, the coin then rests on the left hand tails up. In this trick, the coin always appears to be heads up, giving the impression that it is a double-headed coin.

### The trick

The illusion is created by quick, skilful handling of the coin as the hands make the slapping motion. The diagrams show the moves of the trick in sequence.

**1** Keep the right hand flat and quickly move it from under the heads up coin, without flipping it over.

**2** The coin drops into the left hand, still heads up.

### The double-headed coin trick

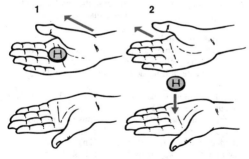

**3** Turn over the right hand as the coin is falling.

**4** The coin lands, still heads up, on the left hand as the right hand slaps down on it.

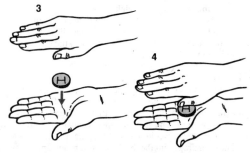

The moves can be repeated from the left hand to the
right hand. The coin does not ever actually turn over,
although it appears to do so because the hands are
making the correct moves to give that illusion.

## Where is the coin?

This trick can be repeated many times and is a good
one to practise before trying more advanced tricks. A
table with a cloth is needed to absorb the sound of a
falling coin.

Place the coin in the palm of one hand with both hands
face up on the table (**1**).

Then turn the hands palm down. As this is done, the
coin is either thrown under the other hand (**2a**) or
retained under the hand that held it (**2b**).

The aim is to make moves **2a** and **2b** look the same so
that when another person is asked to guess which hand
hides the coin (**3**), they have only a 50/50 chance of
guessing correctly (**4**).

### Where is the coin?

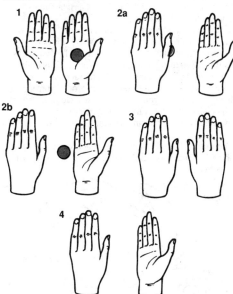

### The French Drop

This is a trick that can be done with a coin, thimble or small ball, using palming to give the illusion that the object has been passed from one hand to the other. It should be practised in front of a mirror.

**1** The object, such as a coin, is held between the thumb and forefinger of the left hand, as the right hand approaches to take it.

**2** The right hand reaches to grasp the coin, which is allowed to slip into the left palm where it is held.

**3** The right hand closes (on nothing) and moves away as if holding the coin, while the left hand falls to the side with the fingers curled in a natural position.

To extend the trick, the coin can be produced from behind the ear or from someone else's clothes. This is especially effective if the coin or object is clearly distinguishable from similar items – e.g. by date or colour.

The French Drop is an impressive and versatile trick. It should be practised until it can be done smoothly with either hand.

**The French Drop**

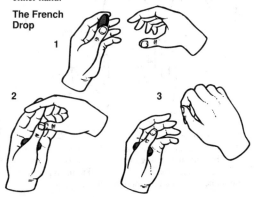

# KNOTS IN ROPE

These are two tricks that need practice with a piece of rope, about 1 m (3½ ft) long. Smooth, fairly heavy but flexible rope can be bought in shops that supply conjuring equipment, but any similar rope can be used. For the first trick, a dab of latex cement will be needed.

## Disappearing knot

Abracadabra! A knot in a piece of rope magically disappears when the rope is pulled tightly.

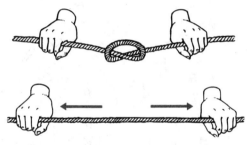

## How to prepare the rope

1 Put two dabs of latex cement on the rope, about 15 cm (6 in) apart.

2 Loop the rope to join the two spots of latex cement together, making sure that rope end **a** is in front of rope end **b**.

3 Pass end **a** through the loop.

4 When ends **a** and **b** are held apart, there appears to be a knot between them. When **a** and **b** are pulled apart, the cement join gives way and the knot disappears.

The trick can be repeated after reconstructing the knot. This can be done in front of an audience because the latex will remain tacky for a while.

## Disappearing knot

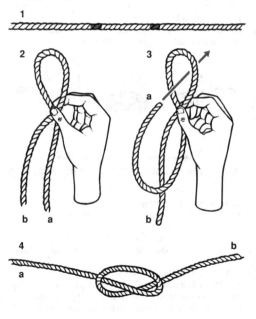

### Producing a knot

Hang the piece of rope (again, about 1 m long) over one
hand. After a quick flick of the wrist, a knot appears in
the rope, as if by magic. Knowing exactly how to hold
the rope and move the hand is the secret of this trick.

1 Place the rope over your left hand, and hold it at point
**x**, between the thumb and forefinger, and at point **y**,
between the ring and little fingers.

2 Quickly bend the hand down, picking up end **a**
between the forefinger and middle finger.

### Producing a knot

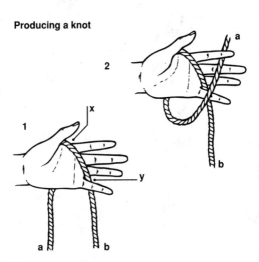

**3** Drop the hand, releasing the rope but retaining a hold on end **a**. Quickly jerk the hand, as though cracking a whip, as this will tighten the knot.

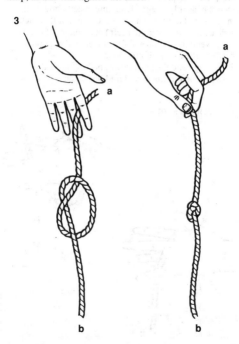

## CARD TRICKS

Magicians often entertain with card tricks, which need to be practised when alone. A new, standard pack of cards, with a border around the back pattern, is the best to use.

The key explains the terms used when describing the tricks.

### Key to card terms

**1** Back of the card, known as "face down".
**2** Face of the card, known as "face up".
**3** and **4** "Top" of the pack or deck.
**5** and **6** "Bottom" of the pack or deck.

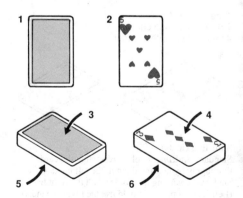

**7** Making a "cut" or "cutting" the cards.
**8** The cut completed.

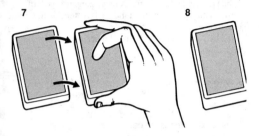

**Types of pack**
**1** Back pattern without a border
**2** Back pattern with a border

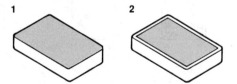

**Shuffling cards**
Standard shuffling involves re-sorting the cards
thoroughly by holding them in the left hand while
randomly changing their order with the right hand.
(Left-handed players would use the reverse hands.)
Quick, facile shuffling should be practised.

**The false shuffle**

It is also possible to give the impression of shuffling while keeping one particular card at the back of the pack.

1 Hold the cards in the normal shuffling position, fingers on the back card (shown shaded) and thumb on the face card.

2 Draw out part of the pack with the right hand while the fingers of the left hand keep the back card in place.

3 Drop the drawn-out cards in front of the remainder of the pack in the left hand, and repeat the action with different numbers of cards being drawn out.

Throughout the shuffle, the left-hand fingers hold onto the back card, always keeping it at the back.

**The false shuffle**

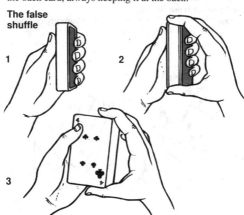

**Palming cards**

Hiding, or palming, cards in the hand is a useful skill when learning card tricks. You do not need large hands to do this well.

**1 Standard palming**

Hold the card, with one of its corners in the flesh at the base of the thumb, and press the top of the card with the fingers slightly bent.

**2 Curled palming**

Hold the lower half of the card against the palm; bend the upper half over and hold it with the thumb.

**3 Back palming**

Hold two corners at the short end of the card firmly between the fingers, as indicated at points **a** and **b**.

**4 Palming from the pack**

Cover the pack with the right hand, apparently squaring the pack, while using the left thumb to push the top card into the right palm, where it is held using standard palming.

## Types of palming

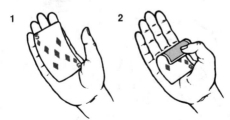

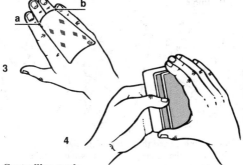

## Controlling cards

Controlling the position of certain cards in the pack, so
that the whereabouts of a particular card is known, is a
skill that takes practice. Skills that control position are
essential to the success of many card tricks.

## The basic hold

The pack of cards should be held in such a way that all
four corners are under control. To do this, hold the pack
in the left hand with the four corners controlled by the
thumb, the base of thumb, the forefinger and the little
finger (1). Left-handed people may prefer to hold the
pack in the right hand.

## The hold when counting cards

When it is necessary to count cards while they are held
in the hand, the basic hold (1) is modified by curling the
forefinger behind the pack (2, 3). This allows greater
control of the pack while the thumb counts cards from
the hidden (back) side, as the pack is slightly bent.

## Counting cards

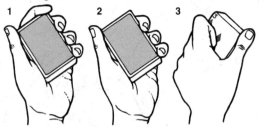

**Controlling a card to the top of the pack**
In this trick, the audience sees a chosen card being
returned to the pack that has been cut, and which is then
cut again. Many card tricks make use of this and similar
methods of control.

The pack of cards should be cut into two parts, **y** and **z**,
before the selected card is returned to it. The holder of
the chosen card is then directed to place it, face down,
onto pile **y** (**1**).

Pile **z** is then placed on pile **y** so that the cards form a
"jog" – i.e. one pile projects over the other (**2**). The
fingers of the left hand will need to be open a little to
allow space for the cards to slide forward slightly to
hide the jog. Then the pack is turned on its side (**3**).
The two piles are still separated by the jog, so that the
right hand can now lift pile **y** (on top of which is the
chosen card) out and place it on the other side of pile **z**
(**4**). Although the audience believe that the chosen card
is in the middle of the pack, the conjuror is able to
produce it, as if by magic, from the top of the pack.

**Controlling a card to the top**

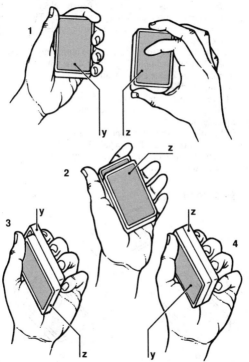

**Forcing a card**

Often a trick relies upon making a person select a card that has already been chosen by the magician. This is known as forcing, and the chosen card is called the "force card".

While the methods for forcing can be quite simple, they should be practised until they can be done with complete confidence and relaxation.

**Forcing by "X-ing" the cut**

1 Place the force card (**a**) on top of the pack.

2 Ask the spectator to cut the pack into two roughly equal sections.

3 The spectator should then be asked to place the bottom half (**c**) across the top half (**b**). (Tell the spectator that placing the cards this way is a reminder of where the pack was cut.)

**X-ing the cut**

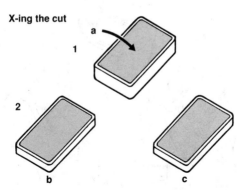

The spectator's attention is distracted at this point with a pleasant piece of conversation, so he or she forgets which half of the pack is which.

**4** The spectator is finally asked to lift the top half (**c**) (originally the bottom half), and to take the top card from the remaining half (**b**), which is the force card (**a**).

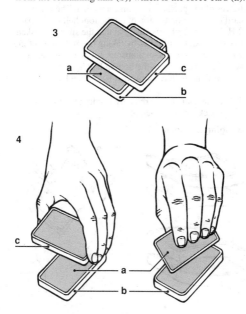

**Forcing by bridging the pack**

This method of making a spectator take a particular
card is not foolproof. It is also used by those who cheat
at card games.

**1** Divide the pack into two roughly equal parts before
the trick is started. Slightly bend the ends of the two
halves of the pack away from each other. The force
card is the one on the top of the bottom half of the pack.

**2** Hold the pack by its sides, so that the spectator asked
to cut the pack will do so by taking the ends and cutting
where the gap has been prepared. Invite the spectator to
take the top card from the bottom half – i.e. the force
card, which you have looked at beforehand and can
name.

**3** Bridging can also be done by bending the two halves
of the pack towards each other.

**Bridging the pack**

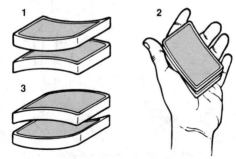

### The glide

This trick uses sleight of hand to produce a named card
from any position in the pack. The magician chooses
the card – e.g. the ace of hearts – which is secretly
already placed underneath the pack of cards (**1**).

A spectator is asked to name any number from 1 to 52.
The magician then draws the stated number of cards
from the bottom of the pack (**2**), the last one of which
will be the ace of hearts.

The magician actually draws the card above the bottom
card each time, while holding back the bottom card –
i.e. the ace of hearts (**3**).

Finally, when the number stated is reached, the ace of
hearts is produced. This is a most impressive trick and
can be repeated many times.

**The glide**

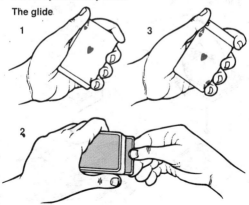

## The magic turnover

**1** The magician names a card – e.g. the 2 of clubs – which has been brought to the top of the pack in readiness. The pack is held face down with the chosen card on top, projecting about 1 cm beyond all the others.

**2** As the pack is dropped, the projecting card resists the flow of air and begins to turn over.

**3** The top card turns over completely as the heavier pack falls.

**4** When the pack finally lands on the ground, the top card – the 2 of clubs – lands last, face up, giving the impression that it has been called out of the pack by magic.

## The magic turnover

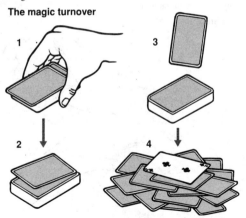

# 3. String games

The intricate knotting and weaving of string on the hands is a very old pastime; it forms part of the culture of many peoples, from the Arctic Eskimos to the Maori of New Zealand, and from the North American Indians to the inhabitants of Papua New Guinea.

## Key to terms

1 thumb
2 forefinger
3 middle finger
4 ring finger
5 little finger
6 front line

7 back thumb lines
8 front forefinger lines
9 back forefinger lines
10 front little finger lines
11 back line
12 reef knot (see overleaf)

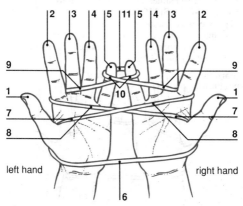

**12**

## EQUIPMENT

You will need a looped piece of strong, pliable string, about 110 cm (44 in) long. If unlooped, it should be long enough to wrap around the knuckles of the hand eight times, and to have its ends joined together with a square or reef knot, thus making a loop.

Traditionally, string patterns are made by one person, although two can take part if the string pattern is slipped onto a partner's hands during a move.

## STARTING POSITIONS

There are two common starting positions.

### Starting position 1

Place the string behind both little fingers, across the palms and behind the thumbs.

**Starting position 1**

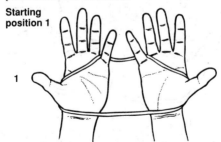

1

Between moves, the normal position of the hands is fingers upwards with palms facing inwards, as in diagram 1. The hands in diagram 2 are turned slightly, to show the string clearly in starting position 1.

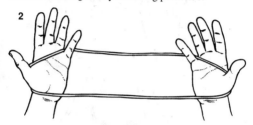

### Starting position 2
1 Loop the string around both forefingers.
2 Push the thumbs between the lines from below.
3 Turn the thumbs down, round and then up, which loops the string around the forefingers and thumbs.
4 Hold out the thumbs so that the string is pulled into two parallel lines.

### Starting position 2

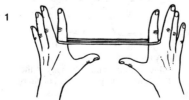

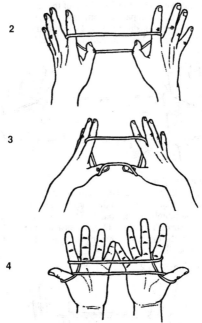

**2**

**3**

**4**

## OPENING MOVES

Some opening moves are the same for many of the
string games, so it is useful to practise and memorise
these openings.

### Opening A

**1** Place the string in starting position 1.
**2** Stretch the fingers out and push the right forefinger under the line which runs across the palm of the left hand.
**3** Pull the string tight.

**Opening A**

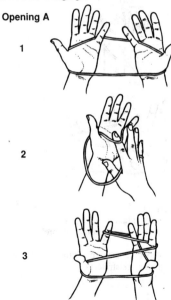

1

2

3

**4** Push the left forefinger under the line which runs across the palm of the right hand.
**5** Pull the string tight.

**Opening A**
(continued)

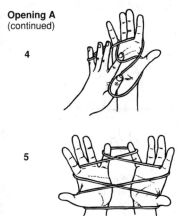

**4**

**5**

**The Murray opening**
**1** Place the string around both forefingers.
**2** Bend the back line between thumbs and forefingers.
**3** Loop the back line.
**4** Push the forefingers together through the loop as the other fingers and thumb are stretched.
**5** Pull the string tight.

## The Murray opening

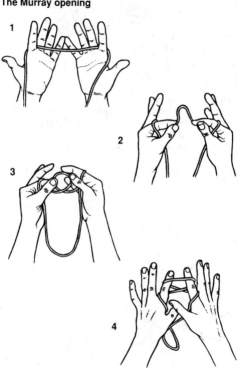

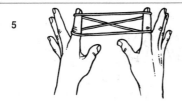

**The Navaho opening**

This opening should not be confused with the Murray opening, although they may appear similar until examined carefully.

1 Loop the string as it is held between the forefingers and thumbs.

2 While holding the string with the other fingers, push both forefingers through the loop from behind.

**The Navaho opening**

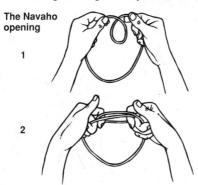

**3** Turn the forefingers down, then up so that they are holding the loop.

**4** Pull the string tight so it is held on the forefingers and the thumbs.

**The Navaho opening** (continued)

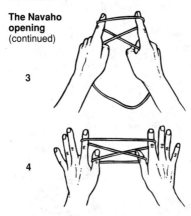

**3**

**4**

## SOME BASIC STRING GAMES

There are hundreds of kinds of string games. The selection described here can all be completed by one person.

### A simple cat's cradle

This is the starting point for many kinds of cat's cradle.

**1** Place the string around the wrists and loop it once round each wrist, keeping the two lines of string parallel.

**2** Push the right forefinger under the line in front of the left wrist. (The middle fingers are sometimes used instead of the forefingers in this and the following step.)

**3** Push the left forefinger under the line in front of the right wrist.

**4** Pull the string tight.

### A simple cat's cradle

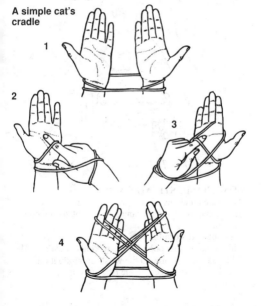

### The ribcage

This is often used as an opening for more complex patterns. It is built from starting position 1 (see p. 110).

**1** Put the lines that are across each palm behind the middle finger of each hand.

**2** Push the right forefinger, from below, under the front forefinger line of the left hand. Then push the right ring finger, from below, under the front ring finger line of the left hand.

**3** Pull the string tight.

**4** The forefinger and ring finger of the left hand then repeat the moves on the right hand. Care must be taken to stay inside the lines.

**5** Pull the string tight again, revealing the ribcage.

### The ribcage

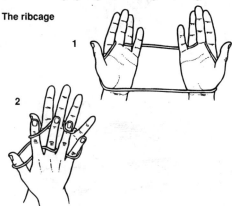

**3**

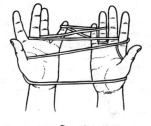

**4**

**5**

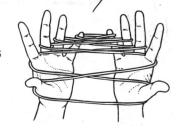

### The cup and saucer

This version was probably first done in New Caledonia. The Salish Indians in western Canada made a similar pattern they called "skinning the bison". The "cup and saucer" is the modern European name.

**1** This pattern begins with opening A (see p. 113).

**2** Bend the thumbs over the crossed lines and under the back forefinger lines.

**3** Then bend the thumbs round and down to pull the back forefinger lines through the front line, so that the front line slips off the thumbs. (This is sometimes called a Navaho Leap, in honour of the skills shown by the nimble-fingered Navaho Indians.)

**The cup and saucer**

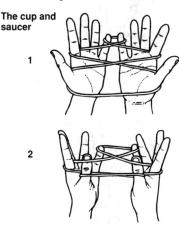

1

2

4 Bend both little fingers forward.
5 Let the string fall off the little fingers.

**The cup and saucer**
(continued)

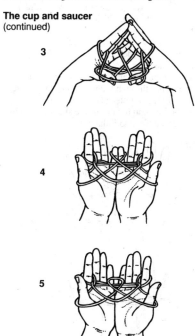

**6** Move the hands apart, pulling the string tight.
**7** Finally, turn the hands to reveal the cup and saucer.

**The cup and saucer**
(continued)

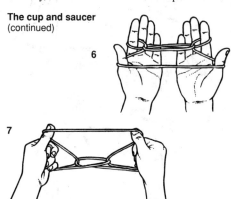

**The fish spear**
**1** The pattern is begun with starting position 1 (see p. 110).
**2** Push the right forefinger under the line across the left palm, pulling and twisting it twice, to form a loop.
**3** Push the left forefinger through this loop and then under the line across the right palm, lifting it up and back through the loop, but not twisting it.
**4** The right thumb and right little finger let go of the string, and the right forefinger pulls the string tight, making the spear.

**The fish spear**

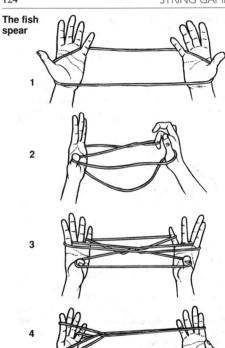

1

2

3

4

### The fly

Known also as the "mosquito" and "smashing the coconut", this game has a surprise ending.

1 Place the string over both thumbs.
2 The right hand lifts both lines over and behind the left hand.
3 Pull the string tight.

**The fly**

**4** From above, hook the little finger of the right hand round the double line at the back of the left hand.
**5** The right little finger then continues to pull the double line from between the forefinger and thumb of the left hand.
**6** The left little finger slides down the right palm, picking up the double line that is hooked on the right thumb.

**The fly**
(continued)

**4**

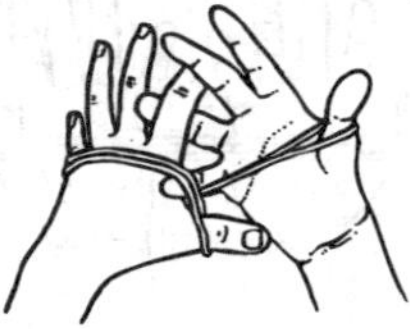

**5**

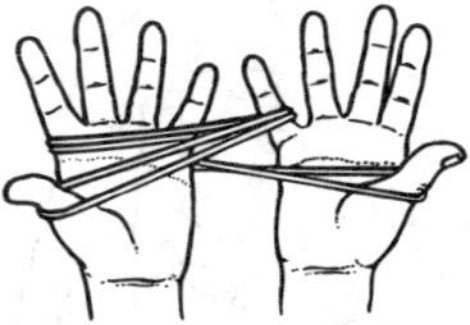

**6**

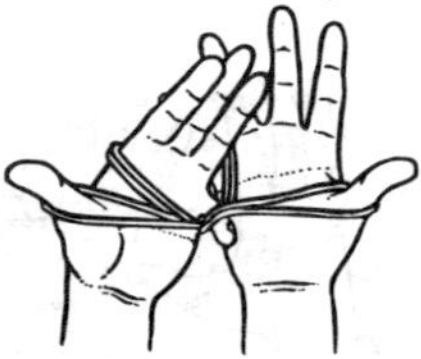

**7** The left little finger continues to pull the double line over the other four lines. The right hand then lifts the double line crossing the left forefinger over the left thumb.

**8** The right hand is used again to lift the double line from behind the left hand, over the left hand, allowing the lines to drop.

**9** Stretch the hands and pull the string to reveal the fly. The final surprise comes when the hands are sharply clapped together, as if to kill the fly, while the loops are dropped off both little fingers. When the string is pulled tight again, the fly disappears and only a loop of string remains between the thumbs, which is how the game started.

**The fly**
(continued)

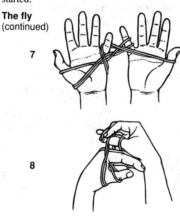

7

8

**9**

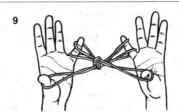

### The thumb-catcher

Most string games make patterns, but some perform tricks. This is one of the latter kind.

**1** The trick begins from starting position 1 (see p. 110) but with the string crossed between the hands. The line from left thumb front to right little finger back should be on top.

**2** As in opening A (see p. 113), push the right forefinger under the line crossing the left palm.

### The thumb-catcher

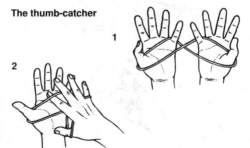

**3** Push the left forefinger under the line crossing the right palm.
**4** Pull the string tight, revealing a pattern similar to opening A, but with an extra line crossing over the palms.
**5** Bend both thumbs down over the forefinger front lines.

**The thumb-catcher**
(continued)

3

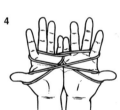

4

5

**6** Push both thumbs down behind the lines, through and up again.

**7** Remove both forefingers and little fingers from the string.

**8** As the hands are opened and the string pulled tight, the thumbs are caught, tied together.

**The thumb-catcher**
(continued)

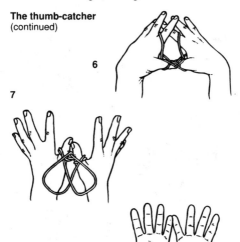

# 4. Solitaire

**TRADITIONAL BOARDS**

Solitaire can be played on either of two types of board. The original French board is octagonal and has 37 holes for pegs made of wood, ivory, bone or plastic. The later English board is circular, has 33 hollows for glass marbles and a groove running around the outer edge to hold eliminated marbles.

**A makeshift board**

The positions can be marked on a piece of strong card and small objects such as dice, counters or hand-made blocks formed from Plasticine can be used instead of marbles or pegs.

**The traditional French board**

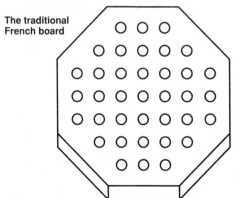

**The traditional English board**

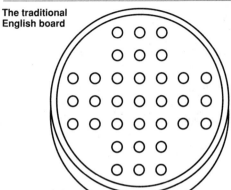

## The aim
Some games require all but one piece to be removed from the board. In others, the objective is to make specific patterns.

## STANDARD SOLITAIRE
The starting positions for the French and English boards are as shown, with all but one hole filled. Usually, the centre hole is left empty but some players choose a different hole.

## Playing
Play begins from the centre of the board (or from the empty hole, if it is not in the centre). A marble (or peg) jumps over a neighbouring marble to fill the empty hole, leaving its own hole empty.

## Starting positions for standard solitaire

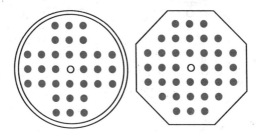

The marble over which it has jumped is eliminated from the game, thus leaving two empty spaces. The game proceeds in this manner until all but one marble remains in the centre of the board.

### Winning a game

A game is completed successfully only if the conditions of play are fulfilled. There may be only one solution, so it is helpful to take note of the moves made.

### VARIATIONS

There are many variations of the standard game and some players enjoy the challenge of inventing their own. Some common variations are described here.

### The cross

This variation is played with only nine pieces. The starting position is a central cross, as shown overleaf. The aim is to eliminate eight pieces, leaving the ninth in the central position.

**Starting positions for the cross**

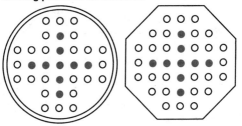

### The corsair

This game is played on the French board, starting with all 37 pegs in place. For the first move, one peg is removed from any of the eight corners or angles, as indicated by the arrows.

The aim is to eliminate all pegs but one, which must remain in the corner opposite the starting corner.

**The eight corners**

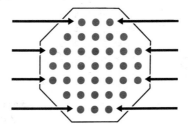

### The first move

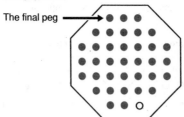

The final peg →

### The octagon

A game on the French board using 29 pegs, leaving all eight corners empty. The aim is to empty the board except for one peg in the centre.

### Starting position for the octagon

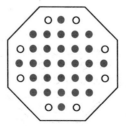

### Patterns on the French board

Many games begin with all 37 pegs in place on the French board. The first peg to be eliminated is the central one. After that, the aim is to remove the pegs until certain patterns are made. Three examples are shown.

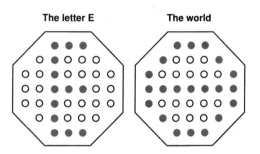

**The letter E**    **The world**

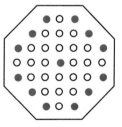

**The apostles**

## SOLUTIONS

Solutions are given to all of the solitaire games described.

**Key to numbers used for the moves**

English board

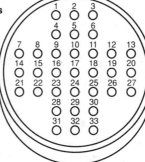

French board

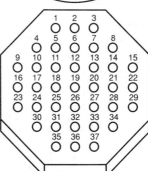

**Standard English solitaire**
Read the moves from left to right along each line, using
the key to identify the numbers.

5–17 12–10 3–11 18–6 1–3 3–11 30–18 27–25
24–26 13–27 27–25 22–24 31–23 16–28 33–31
31–23 4–16 7–9 10–8 21–7 7–9 24–10 10–8 8–22
22–24 24–26 19–17 16–18 11–25 26–24 29–17

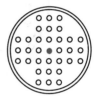

**Standard French solitaire**
6–19 4–6 18–5 6–4 9–11 24–10 11–9 26–24 35–25
24–26 27–25 33–31 25–35 29–27 14–28 27–29
19–21 7–20 21–19

**The English cross**

10–2 24–10 15–17 17–5 19–17 2–10 10–24 29–17

**The French cross**

12–2 26–12 17–19 19–6 21–19 2–12 12–26 32–19

**The corsair**

35–37 26–36 25–35 23–25 34–32 20–33 37–27
7–20 20–33 18–31 35–25 5–18 18–31 29–27
22–20 15–13 16–18 9–11 20–7 7–5 4–6 18–5 1–11
33–20 20–18 18–5 5–7 36–26 30–32 32–19 19–6
2–12 8–6 12–2 3–1

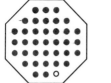 

## The octagon

27–37 31–33 37–27 20–33 22–20 19–32 33–31
30–32 36–26 17–30 26–24 30–17 34–21 21–19
18–20 16–18 8–21 21–19 7–20 11–25 20–18 25–11
11–13 2–12 13–11 10–12 4–6 6–19

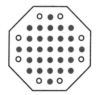 

## The letter E

32–19 34–32 20–33 29–27 35–20 36–26 30–32
26–36 18–31 20–18 7–20 15–13 20–7 22–20 6–19
4–6 18–5 23–25 16–17 9–11 2–12 8–6 12–2

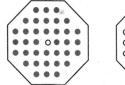 

**The world**

32–19 30–32 17–30 28–26 25–27 14–28 34–21
32–34 4–17 6–4 18–5 13–11 5–18 27–13 7–20

**The apostles**

32–19 28–26 37–27 35–37 25–35 27–25 24–26
11–25 25–27 16–18 19–17 6–19 4–6 17–4 2–12
8–6 2–7 6–8 22–20 15–13 12–14 23–13 13–15

# 5. Tangrams

A tangram is a two-dimensional pattern made using all seven parts of a square that has been divided according to tradition.

**THE TRADITIONAL DIVISION OF THE SQUARE**

The basic tangram is not less than 15 cm (6 in) square and is divided, as shown, into seven parts:

    2 large triangles;
    1 medium triangle;
    2 small triangles;
    1 square;
    1 parallelogram.

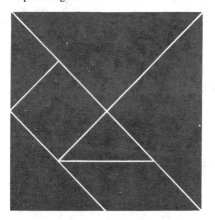

The parts of the tangram are known as the seven tans.
The game originated in China, before 1800, but the
name "tangram" may have European origins.

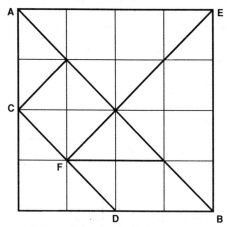

## HOW TO MAKE THE BASIC TANGRAM

A 15 cm (6 in) square of cardboard, picture mounting
board or wood, not more than 6 mm (¹/₄ in) thick, are
ideal. The wood can be painted or coloured paper can
be stuck on the cardboard if desired, but the overall
effect should be of one colour.

### Drawing and cutting the seven tans

Using light lines drawn with a sharp pencil and ruler,
divide the surface into 16 equal squares. The heavy

lines, marking the shapes of the seven tans, can then be constructed accurately, as follows: the diagonal A to B; the line C to D; the line E to F; a line from C, diagonally across the small square, to meet the line AB; a line from F, along the sides of two small squares to meet AB. The board or wood should then be cut along these lines, with a sharp craft knife or jig-saw, and each tan carefully sanded so that the edges are smooth to the touch.

When complete, the seven tans should fit snugly together to make the basic square again.

**The seven tans**

## PLAYING TANGRAMS

Making tangrams demands patience, imagination and a sense of humour. It is possible to make some 1,600 different patterns. All seven tans should be used for each pattern and kept flat, in one plane. There are three categories of patterns: invented shapes; reproduced shapes; and constructed shapes.

### Inventing shapes

The player invents as many shapes as possible, silhouettes of animals, people, objects, etc.

**Buildings**

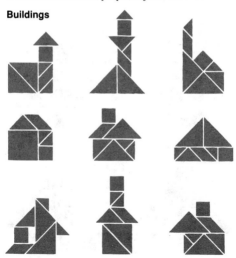

**Boats**

**Animals 1**

**Animals 2**

**People 1**

**People 2**

**Reproducing shapes**

The player attempts to reproduce given silhouettes.
Here are some tangrams to reproduce. The solutions
begin on p. 155.

**Letters and numbers**

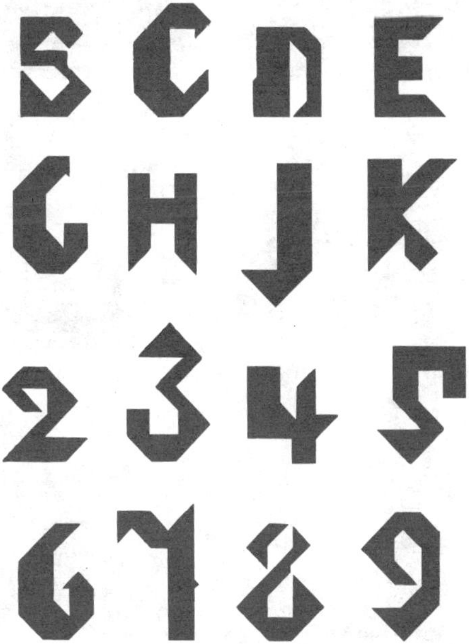

**Buildings**

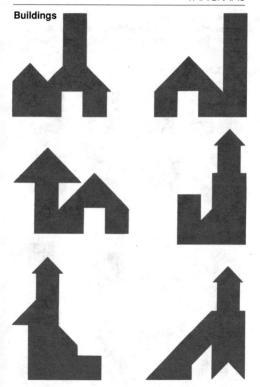

**Shapes**

**People**

**Solutions**

**Constructing shapes**

This is a geometrical activity in which the player attempts to make given shapes, e.g.:

a rectangle;
a right-angled triangle (one angle is 90 degrees);
a four-sided shape, neither square nor rectangle;
a five-sided shape; or
a six-sided shape.

Here are some shapes to try to construct. The solutions begin on p. 159.

**Solutions**

# 6. Word games

There are many absorbing word games. A selection for playing alone are described here with some challenges. Solutions, where appropriate, are listed at the end of this chapter.

## ACROSTICS

The first letter of each line of a poem or rhyme spells out a name, word or phrase. In a double acrostic, both first and last letters spell out a word and, in a triple acrostic, the middle letters also make a word or phrase.

### A London acrostic

This sample acrostic builds the name **London** with the first letter of each line.

> **L**ively city
> **O**ld buildings
> **N**ew ideas
> **D**ungeons in the Tower
> **O**ld Father Thames
> **N**ever a dull moment

A double acrostic using the name **London**:

> **L**ooking lively and full
> **O**ne great big zoo
> **N**o shortage of people out to win
> **D**elighted and excited
> **O**pen all night too.
> **N**obody had such fun

### A Latin acrostic

An acrostic may also be a complete word square, such as the Roman acrostic found during excavations at Pompeii: *sator arepo tenet opera rotas*, which roughly translates from the Latin as "the wheels are carefully guided by Arepo, the sower".

```
S A T O R  when reversed, reads as  R O T A S
A R E P O                           O P E R A
T E N E T                           T E N E T
O P E R A                           A R E P O
R O T A S                           S A T O R
```

### Challenges

**1** Describe a place with an acrostic poem or rhyme.

**2** Use your own full name to build an acrostic list of likes and dislikes, virtues and vices, etc. Similar acrostics can be made for family or friends.

## ALPHABET GAMES

A common activity is to make an alphabet poem using the letters of the alphabet to start the lines or verses. This children's alphabet dates from the early 17th century.

**A** was an apple-pie,
**B** bit it,
**C** cut it,
**D** dealt it,
**E** eyed it,
**F** fought for it,
**G** got it,
**H** had it,
**I** inspected it,

**J** jumped for it,
**K** kept it,
**L** longed for it,
**M** mourned for it,
**N** nodded at it,
**O** opened it,
**P** peeped at it,
**Q** quartered it,
**R** ran for it,
**S** stole it,
**T** took it,
**U** upset it,
**V** viewed it,
**W** wanted it,
**X**, **Y**, **Z** and ampersand
All wished for a piece in hand.

### A Victorian alphabet game

"The parson's cat" is a party game but it can easily be
adapted to make an alphabet poem, which might begin
like this:

> The parson's cat is an active cat,
> And his name is Archibald. He's
> Bouncy,
> Cunning,
> Daring,
> Exciting, and
> Frets if he can't have his way.
> Gambolling off on a summer's day,
> He . . . .

and so on, each line using the next letter in the
alphabet.

**The travelling alphabet**

This time the poem starts with the name of a country or place beginning with A. A description of what was (or will be) done there is added, also using the letter A. The next line deals with a place beginning with B and a description, and so on through the alphabet. For example, a travelling alphabet poem might begin like this:

> In Amsterdam, I ate an apple,
> In Blackpool, I bought big, brown bears,
> In Cologne, I chased chickens,
> In Dallas, I drew ducks,
> And in . . . .

and so on.

Here is a list of countries and places that will be helpful in playing the game. It is also an idea for the player to use places that have been visited recently or in the past.

**A** Amsterdam, Africa, Angelsey, Australia
**B** Blackpool, Bulgaria, Brazil, Bristol
**C** Cologne, Cyprus, Canada, Cardiff
**D** Dallas, Denmark, Dulwich, Dumfries
**E** England, Enfield, Edinburgh, Exeter
**F** France, Fulham, Florida, Frankfurt
**G** Germany, Glasgow, Gwent, Granada
**H** Hungary, Honduras, Hong Kong, Hawaii
**I** Italy, Ireland, India, Ipswich
**J** Japan, Jamaica, Jerusalem, Jersey
**K** Kuwait, Kettering, Kingston, Kent
**L** Luxembourg, Lisbon, Liverpool, Leith
**M** Manchester, Madrid, Mexico, Malaysia
**N** New Zealand, Newquay, Norway, Netherlands
**O** Oxford, Ohio, Oslo, Ontario
**P** Portugal, Preston, Pennsylvania, Poland

**Q** Queensland, Quebec, Queens, Qatar
**R** Rickmansworth, Russia, Ronçeval, Romania
**S** Spain, Southampton, St Ives, San Marino
**T** Taiwan, Tahiti, Tokyo, Turkey
**U** Uganda, Utrecht, Uruguay, USA
**V** Vienna, Valencia, Victoria, Versailles
**W** Wrexham, Weston-super-Mare, Waterloo, Washington
**X** Xuyong, Xiji, Xuanhan, Xochmilco
**Y** Yugoslavia, Yorkshire, Yemen, Yukon
**Z** Zagreb, Zambia, Zaïre, Zaragoza

## Alphabet categories

This game is a real memory-tester. A word with five or six different letters is chosen at random, such as **person**, **crawl** or **place**, and written across a page.

Then five or six categories of nouns are selected and written down the left-hand side. The categories could be animals, plants, machines, places, books, transport, food, etc.

The aim is then to use the letter at the top of each column as the initial letter of the nouns in the given categories. It is often more challenging to work against the clock or to use very specific categories such as French wines, gaseous elements, etc.

### Example of a completed category game

|        | **P** | **E** | **R** | **S** | **O** | **N** |
|--------|-------|-------|-------|-------|-------|-------|
| place  | Peru  | Eire  | Rome  | Seoul | Ohio  | New York |
| plant  | poppy | endive | reed | soya  | orpine | nemesia |
| colour | pink  | ecru  | red   | sepia | ochre | navy |
| food   | plum  | egg   | ragout | soup | orange | noodles |
| wood   | pine  | elm   | redwood | sycamore | oak | nutmeg-tree |

**Challenges**

**1** Build an alphabet poem from "A is for art".

**2** Construct a local travelling alphabet.

**3** Make an alphabet, like "the parson's cat", based on a cat called Agatha.

**4** Choose six categories and use the word **answer** to fill the spaces in the columns below.

| categories | A | N | S | W | E | R |
|---|---|---|---|---|---|---|
| 1 | . | . | . | . | . | . |
| 2 | . | . | . | . | . | . |
| 3 | . | . | . | . | . | . |
| 4 | . | . | . | . | . | . |
| 5 | . | . | . | . | . | . |
| 6 | . | . | . | . | . | . |

## ANAGRAMS

A favourite of crossword puzzle makers, an anagram is the rearrangement of the letters of a word or phrase to make a new word or phrase, e.g. **male** becomes **meal**; **groan** becomes **organ**; and **ladies** becomes **ideals**. Some words have more than one anagram, such as **salesmen** which can be transformed into **lameness**, **maleness** and **nameless**.

An Edinburgh newspaper once printed a story containing 50 anagrammatic phrases of the word **monastery**, such as **nasty Rome**, **money arts** and **stone Mary**.

An anagram can consist of several words, e.g. **disappointment** becomes **made in pint pots**; **the eyes** becomes **they see**; and **astronomers** becomes **moon-starers**.

**How to find the anagram of a word**
It can be helpful to rearrange the available letters so the
eyes can scan them and construct new words more
easily.
For example, to find an anagram of the word
**medication** the letters can be placed either in a circle

or spread out randomly, as below.

ADEICIOTNM

This may help to find the anagram, **decimation**.

**Appropriate anagrams**
Purists insist that the anagram should always be
appropriate, i.e. it should have a similar meaning to the
original word or phrase, e.g. **angered** is an anagram of
**enraged**; **train** is an anagram of **it ran**; **conversation**
is an anagram of **voices rant on**.
The *Boy's Own Book* of 1828 lists several appropriate
anagrams.

GOLDEN LAND . . . OLD ENGLAND
RARE MAD FROLIC . . . RADICAL REFORM
PARISHIONERS . . . I HIRE PARSONS

Appropriate anagrams can be made from names, e.g.
**Margaret Thatcher** can be an anagram of **that great
charmer** or of **Meg the arch-tartar**; **Piet Modrian** is

an anagram of **I paint modern**, which he did; **Clint
Eastwood** appropriately forms the anagram **Old West
action**. Lewis Carroll's anagram of **Florence
Nightingale** was **flit on, cheering angel**.

### Name anagrams

Pseudonyms can be anagrams of a person's real name,
for example, in 1981 **Richard Stilgoe** wrote a book of
stories about fictional people whose names were all
anagrams of his own, including **Sir Eric Goldhat**;
**Giscard O'Hitler**; and **Dr Gloria Ethics**.

### Anagram pairs

Anagram pairs are two-word solutions which are
anagrams of each other and which are derived from a
clue.

> **clue** sea-going craft
> **solution** ocean canoe

**Ocean** and **canoe** are anagrams of each other.

### Antigrams

Antigrams are anagrams with an opposite meaning.
Examples are given below.

> RESTFUL . . . FLUSTER
> UNITED . . . UNTIED
> SANTA . . . SATAN
> ROME WAS NOT BUILT IN A DAY . . . ANY
> LABOUR I DO WANTS TIME

### More anagram solutions

Anagram puzzle verses might appeal to the really
dedicated anagram maker. Hubert Phillips wrote
several, one of which is

"The ——— are terribly small,"
Say I to my wife in the hall.
Her big ——— eyes
Open wide: she replies:
"It was ——— I ordered, that's all."

The missing words, all anagrams of each other, are
**melons, solemn** and **lemons**.

### Challenges

**1** Make an anagram word or phrase from each word
listed.

    **a** Abominable
    **b** Causal
    **c** Desperation
    **d** Endearments
    **e** Infection
    **f** Martial
    **g** Punishment
    **h** Softheartedness
    **i** Therapeutics

**2** Make 50 or more anagrammatic words or phrases
from the word **monastery**.

**3** Try to make anagrams from your name or the names
of members of your family.

**4** Solve the clues, from Tony Auguarde's *Word Games*,
below. The answers are two words which are anagrams
of each other, e.g.

    **clue** hidden promise
    **solution** latent talent

    **a** Drink fit for a king.
    **b** Object in outer space.
    **c** Bring back the visitor.

   **d** A drummer in Concord.

   **e** Marks and Spencer making gold.

   **f** Race-course cadet.

The solutions to this challenge are at the end of the chapter.

## CROSSWORDS

A crossword puzzle is a set of clues which, when solved, produce words that fit into the "lights" or blank squares of a crossword grid.

The grid is usually made up of lights and black squares. The positions of the words are marked with numbers that correspond with those of the clues.

Most newspapers and magazines regularly publish crossword puzzles, and many are collected in paperback books.

The crossword puzzle presented here is thought to be the first "word-cross" puzzle. It was made by a Liverpool journalist called Arthur Wynne, who emigrated to New York. He published it in the *New York World* on 21 December 1913. It was an instant success, and a month later the name was changed to "crossword" puzzle.

### Challenge

Solve Arthur Wynne's word-cross puzzle, which was on the "Fun" page of the newspaper. His solution has not been recorded, so one has been suggested at the end of this chapter.

The clues are numbered to correspond with the numbers at either end of each line of the grid.

Note: while most of the meanings and spellings of the
words are still common today, some words may not be
familiar because the word-cross was created in 1913.
The spelling of certain words, such as **fiber**, is
American, and the spelling of **gomutti** is the old-
fashioned spelling.

### The word-cross puzzle

clues across

**2–3** What bargain
hunters enjoy.

**4–5** A written
acknowledgement.

**6–7** Such and nothing
more.

**8–9** To cultivate.

**10–11** A bird.

**12–13** A bar of wood or
iron.

**14–15** Opposed to less.

clues down

**10–18** The fiber of the
gomutti palm.

**6–22** What we all
should be.

**4–26** A daydream.

**2–11** A talon.

**19–28** A pigeon.

**F–7** Part of your head.

**23–30** A river in Russia.

**16–17** What artists learn
to do.

**18–19** What this puzzle
is.

**20–21** Fastened.

**22–23** An animal of prey.

**24–25** Found on the
seashore.

**26–27** The close of a day.

**28–29** To elude.

**30–31** The plural of is.

**1–32** To govern.

**33–34** A police informer.

**N–8** A fist.

**24–31** To agree with.

**3–12** Part of a ship.

**20–29** One.

**5–27** Exchanging.

**9–25** To sink in mud.

**13–21** A boy.

```
                    1
               F  U  N
          2              3
       4           32        5
       6        7     8        9
   10        11        12        13
14        15           16        17
   18        19        20     21
      22        23     24     25
         26     33        27
            28        29
            30     31
               34
```

## DOUBLETS

This is a letter game invented by Lewis Carroll which he had published in *Vanity Fair* in 1879. A doublet consists of two related words containing the same number of letters, e.g. **head** and **tail** are a doublet. The aim of the game is to find "link" words to complete a chain which transforms **head** into **tail**. Each link word is provided by changing only one letter of the previous word.

```
HEAD
HEAL
TEAL
TELL
TALL
TAIL
```

Anagrams may be used, but only as a separate step.

## Scoring

Lewis Carroll also invented a scoring system:
**a** count the number of letters in the first word and add 1;
**b** multiply this number by itself;
**c** deduct two points from the square number for every link word. This is the final score.

## Sample scoring

The doublet **cat–dog** might be linked thus:

```
CAT
COT
DOT
DOG
```

The score would be

**a** 3 + 1 = 4
**b** 4 x 4 = 16
**c** 16 – 4 (two link words) = 12

## Challenges

Try to make link words for the examples given below.
**1** Lewis Carroll's doublets, published in 1879:
**a ape** to **man** in not more than six moves; and
**b iron** to **lead**, using an anagram for one of the links.
**2** Professor Haffmann's doublets, published in *Transformations* in 1893:
**a black** to **white**, making a chain of nine words; and
**b hand** to **foot** in not more than seven moves.
**3** J. E. Surrick and L. M. Conant's difficult doublet, published in *Laddergrams* in 1927:
**small** to **large**.
The chain of this last doublet will need a minimum of fifteen moves (14 link words).

There are no right or wrong ways to link doublets, but some methods are offered in the solutions section.
Here are some other doublets that offer a challenge. No solutions are suggested.

    LIVE–DEAD
    LOVE–HATE
    MORE–LESS
    MAN–BOY
    SEVEN–EIGHT (another long chain)

## PALINDROMES

A word or phrase, which can be read exactly the same backwards as it can be read forwards, is called a palindrome. The words **peep** and **noon** are palindromes.
Phrases and sentences can also be palindromes, such as the examples given below.

    able was I ere I saw Elba
    live not on evil
    Adam I'm Ada

### Challenges

Find the one-word palindromes that fit these clues. The number of letters in the palindrome is given in brackets after each clue.

**1** Compositions for one voice or instrument (5).
**2** Something done (4).
**3** Men and women are the two of them (5).
**4** She has taken holy orders (3).
**5** Paste it on the wall again (7).
**6** To consult another source of information (5).
**7** Lengthy old stories (5).
**8** Not sloping or uneven (5).

## PANGRAMS

A pangram is a sentence that contains all 26 letters of
the alphabet. The aim is to keep the total number of
letters as low as possible.

One of the best known pangrams, to typists at least, is
the practice sentence below.

> the quick brown fox jumps over the lazy dog

This pangram has a total of 35 letters, containing three
Es, two Hs, four Os, two Us and two Ts.

### Other examples of pangrams

> by Jove, my quick study of lexicography won
> a prize (41 letters)
> the five boxing wizards jump quickly (31 letters)

### Challenge

There are hundreds of possible pangrams. The shorter
they are the harder it is to make sense of them. Try to
make some original ones, using less than 50 letters.

## WORD SQUARES

A word square contains words of equal length that read
the same way both horizontally and vertically. Most
commonly, the words are the same in both directions.
In the rarer double-word squares, the horizontal words
are different from the vertical ones.

### Some common word squares

```
MAN     CREW     CREST
ATE     RAVE     REACH
NET     EVER     EAGER
        WERE     SCENE
                 THREE
```

```
C I R C L E
I C A R U S
R A R E S T
C R E A T E
L U S T R E
E S T E E M
```

**A double-word square**

```
O R A L
M A R E
E V E N
N E A T
```

Seven-word squares are more difficult; the puzzle expert, H. E. Dudney, who died in 1930, made several, including this one.

```
N E S T L E S
E N T R A N T
S T R A N G E
T R A I T O R
L A N T E R N
E N G O R G E
S T E R N E R
```

Eight-word squares usually require some unusual words or names. Modern experts have claimed that up to 900 nine-word squares have been made and even some of 10 words. A large dictionary and a gazetteer are essential to research the obscure words that would be necessary to complete such squares.

Since words with a high proportion of vowels are needed to build large word squares, tautonyms are sometimes useful. A tautonym is a word that consists of a word repeated, for example, **tangatanga** and **galangalan**.

## Other word shapes

The words in the diamond and triangle below can be read both horizontally and vertically.

```
        L                P A R R O T
      S E T              A L O O F
    S C O R E            R O O T
  L E O P A R D          R O T
    T R A C E            O F
      E R E              T
        D
```

diamond              triangle

## Challenges

Try to construct word squares. Start with three-letter words and work upwards. Here are two ways of starting.

**1** Choose a word and place it in its horizontal and vertical positions. For example, the word **prepare** can be used to make word squares. Try several starting positions.

```
P R E P A R E          . . . . . . P
R . . . . . .          . . . . . . R
E . . . . . .          . . . . . . E
P . . . . . .          . . . . . . P
A . . . . . .          . . . . . . A
R . . . . . .          . . . . . . R
E . . . . . .          P R E P A R E
```

top and left position    bottom and right position

```
. . . P . . .
. . . R . . .
. . . E . . .
P R E P A R E
. . . A . . .
. . . R . . .
. . . E . . .
```

central position

**2** Open a book at random and pick any sentence. Use the first four letters of the sentence as the centre of the word square. Then try to build a four- or six-word square around them. For example, the first four letters of this paragraph are O, P, E and N.

```
. . . .        . . . . . .
. O P .        . . . . . .
. E N .        . . O P . .
. . . .        . . E N . .
               . . . . . .
               . . . . . .
```

## WORD QUIZZES

Many people enjoy a quiz, so here are a few. The solutions are given at the end of this chapter.

### Pairs

An easy start. Some words and names have natural partners. Add the word that completes the pair.

1 Stars and
2 Jack and
3 Romulus and
4 Antony and
5 Tristan and
6 Samson and
7 Frankie and
8 Laurel and
9 Gog and
10 The lion and

| 11 Brimstone and | 17 Cat and |
|---|---|
| 12 Tweedledum and | 18 Hengist and |
| 13 Tooth and | 19 Hansel and |
| 14 Sackcloth and | 20 Fortnum and |
| 15 Black and | 21 William and |
| 16 Spick and | 22 Rogers and |

## Making words

**1** Write 20 words beginning with colours, e.g. **redundant** and **blacksmith**.

**2** Find 20 words ending in **ship**, e.g. **worship**.

**3** Find 20 words containing the letters T, I and N, in that order, and not ending in **ing**; e.g. **tint**.

## Jumbled occupations

The letters of the names of different jobs have been mixed up. Rearrange the letters to find out what they are, e.g. **trocod** reads **doctor**. A double jumble makes two words.

| 1 Icaption | 11 Cactonnaut |
|---|---|
| 2 Neeringe | 12 Brumple |
| 3 Priestnotice | 13 Colipe ffierco |
| 4 Mashtinic | 14 Gaste armange |
| 5 Reachet | 15 Teeviceux |
| 6 Chistrypista | 16 Cacritthe |
| 7 Riccle | 17 Freesu cloctrole |
| 8 Grueson | 18 Spoasselern |
| 9 Corpetum | 19 Tiorirne corotrade |
| morrgrapem | 20 Pleascand greensid |
| 10 Melvilrhisst | |

## Words ending in "ation"

The answers to the clues are all words ending with the letters A, T, I, O and N.

1 Political murder
2 Additional growth
3 Cultural development
4 Sharing the news
5 Entanglement
6 Removal of salt
7 Movement off normal course
8 Learning for life
9 The arrangement of windows
10 Induced proposition
11 An illusion
12 Embodiment
13 Joining parts to make a whole
14 Rising without visible support
15 Act of chewing
16 Qualifying examination
17 Received notice
18 Fate; preordained salvation
19 Ready-made in sections
20 Act in a way that is misleading
21 Delaying action
22 Giving up office
23 Bringing back to former condition
24 Progress held back
25 Chewing of the cud
26 A physical consciousness
27 Sluggish condition
28 Agitated alarm

### Decoding words

The letters of each word are numbered from 1 upwards.
A description of the word, and clues to shorter words
that use the same numbers, will reveal the letters. For
example, **elephant** would be numbered thus:

**E L E P H A N T**
**1 2 3 4 5 6 7 8**

Clues might be, e.g.

An animal
**a** 2, 3, 6, 4, a jump – **LEAP**
**b** 5, 6, 8, worn on the head – **HAT**

The letters L, E, P, H, A and T are given, from which **elephant** can be completed. The aim is to guess the word without having to use all the clues.

**1** Power

    **a** 12, 2, 4, a hole in the ground.

    **b** 6, 8, 5, 2, 4, 7, 8, someone treacherous.

    **c** 9, 10, 2, 12, a sailing vessel.

**2** Theft or incorrect use of an object

    **a** 3, 4, 5, rises in plants.

    **b** 16, 12, 13, 14, 15, 16, the people of a country.

    **c** 6, 8, 9, 3, corn does it when hot.

**3** Part of character

    **a** 1, 4, 5, Greek letter P.

    **b** 3, 5, 8, complement of yang.

    **c** 10, 11, belongs to me.

**4** Earthly

    **a** 4, 5, 6, 1, wine for ships?

    **b** 4, 2, 7, round vegetable.

    **c** 1, 2, 7, 3, group working together.

## SOLUTIONS

### Anagrams

**4a** Regal lager

  **b** Remote meteor

  **c** Recall caller

  **d** Supersonic percussion

  **e** St Michael's alchemists

  **f** Aintree trainee

**Crosswords**

**Word-cross puzzle**

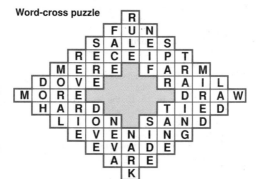

**Doublets**

**1a** Ape–are–ere–err–ear–mar–man (there is a 5-step version too)

**b** Iron–icon–coin–corn–cord–lord–load–lead

**2a** Black–slack–stack–stalk–stale–shale–whale–while–white

**b** Hand–hard–lard–lord–ford–fort–foot

**3** Small–stall–still–spill–spile–spine–seine–seise–sense–tense–terse–verse–verge–merge–marge–large

**Palindromes**

**1** Solos

**2** Deed

**3** Sexes

**4** Nun

**5** Repaper

**6** Refer

**7** Sagas

**8** Level

**Word quizzes**

**Pairs**

| | | | |
|---|---|---|---|
| 1 | Stripes | 12 | Tweedledee |
| 2 | Jill | 13 | Nail |
| 3 | Remus | 14 | Ashes |
| 4 | Cleopatra | 15 | White (or blue) |
| 5 | Iseult | 16 | Span |
| 6 | Delilah | 17 | Mouse |
| 7 | Johnny | 18 | Horsa |
| 8 | Hardy | 19 | Gretel |
| 9 | Magog | 20 | Mason |
| 10 | The unicorn | 21 | Mary |
| 11 | Treacle | 22 | Hammerstein |

**Making words**

1 Blackbird, blackguard, blacking, blackout, bluebeard, bluebottle, blueprint, brownie, brownshirt, greenery, greenfinger, greengage, greengrocer, greenhouse, greyhound, greylag, indigolite, orangery, pinkie, pinking, redeem, redolent, redoubt, redress, reduce.

2 Comradeship, fellowship, friendship, hardship, partnership, scholarship, spaceship, steamship, stewardship, warship.

3 Concertina, continent, continue, gelatine, guillotine, impertinent, itinerant, nicotine, nightingale, retina, routine, satin, serpentine, stint, tincture, tinder, tinker, tinkle, tinnitus, tinsel, tint, tiny, tintinnabulation.

**Jumbled occupations**

| | | | |
|---|---|---|---|
| 1 | Optician | 5 | Teacher |
| 2 | Engineer | 6 | Psychiatrist |
| 3 | Receptionist | 7 | Cleric |
| 4 | Machinist | 8 | Surgeon |

9 Computer
    programmer
10 Silversmith
11 Accountant
12 Plumber
13 Police officer
14 Stage manager

15 Executive
16 Architect
17 Refuse collector
18 Salesperson
19 Interior decorator
20 Landscape designer

## Words ending in "ation"

1 Assassination
2 Augmentation
3 Civilisation
4 Communication
5 Complication
6 Desalination
7 Deviation
8 Education
9 Fenestration
10 Generalisation
11 Hallucination
12 Incarnation
13 Integration
14 Levitation

15 Mastication
16 Matriculation
17 Notification
18 Predestination
19 Prefabrication
20 Prevarication
21 Procrastination
22 Resignation
23 Restoration
24 Retardation
25 Rumination
26 Sensation
27 Stagnation
28 Trepidation

## Decoding words

1 Dictatorship
a Pit
b Traitor
c Ship
2 Misappropriation
a Sap
b Nation
c Pops

3 Physiognomy
a Psi
b Yin
c My
4 Temporal
a Port
b Pea
c Team

# 7. Number puzzles

In this section are a selection of activities for those who enjoy playing with numbers.

**FINGER CALCULATIONS**

Using the fingers of the right hand to count units and the left-hand fingers to count tens, addition and

## Numerical value of fingers

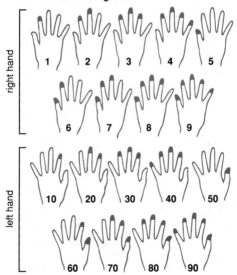

subtraction up to 99 can be done. Skilled operators can
compute as quickly with their fingers as with an
electronic calculator, without having to look at their
hands.

## Addition

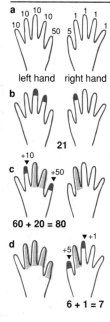

**a**
left hand  right hand

**b**
21

**c**
+10  +50
60 + 20 = 80

**d**
+5  +1
6 + 1 = 7

**a** When adding numbers, e.g.
21 + 66 = 87, remember that,
on the left hand, each finger
has a value of 10, and that the
thumb has a value of 50. On
the right hand, each finger
carries a value of 1 and the
thumb has a value of 5.
**b** First, the shaded fingers are
pressed down, indicating the
value of 21.
**c** Then the tens (60) of 66 are
added. Here, the left-hand
thumb is pressed down, adding
50; then the ring finger of the
left hand is pressed down,
adding another 10. Thus, on the
left hand, three fingers (total,
30) and the thumb (equal to 50)
are pressed down: the total on
the left hand is now 80.
**d** To add the units (6), the right-
hand thumb is pressed down,
adding 5; then the middle
finger of the right hand is
pressed down, another 1.

Two fingers (totalling 2) and the thumb (equal to 5) are pressed down: the total on the right hand is now 7.

**e** When the totals of both hands are put together, the sum is 87.

## Subtraction

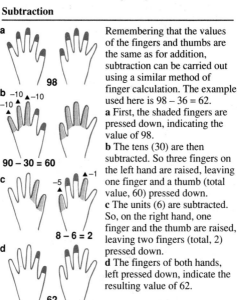

Remembering that the values of the fingers and thumbs are the same as for addition, subtraction can be carried out using a similar method of finger calculation. The example used here is 98 – 36 = 62.

**a** First, the shaded fingers are pressed down, indicating the value of 98.

**b** The tens (30) are then subtracted. So three fingers on the left hand are raised, leaving one finger and a thumb (total value, 60) pressed down.

**c** The units (6) are subtracted. So, on the right hand, one finger and the thumb are raised, leaving two fingers (total, 2) pressed down.

**d** The fingers of both hands, left pressed down, indicate the resulting value of 62.

## Multiplication

Two methods are shown, the first is suitable only for
some calculations in the decimal system, i.e. base ten.
The second method can be used for any base.

### Method 1

This method can be used to multiply any two numbers
between 5 and 10 in the decimal system, e.g. $6 \times 8$.

**a** Subtract 5 from the first number, noting the difference
by lifting one finger on the left hand: $6 - 5 = 1$.

**b** Subtract 5 from the second number, noting the
difference by lifting three fingers on the right hand:
$8 - 5 = 3$.

Add the number of fingers, $1 + 3 = 4$. This indicates the
number of tens in the product, i.e. 4 tens (40).

**c** To find the units, count the number of folded fingers
on each hand and multiply them together: $4 \times 2 = 8$.
(The thumbs count as fingers.)

The product of $6 \times 8$ is made up of 4 tens and 8 units,
i.e. 48.

**Multiplication:
method 1**

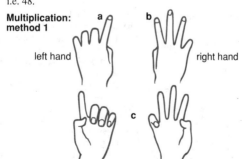

left hand                                    right hand

### Method 2

This method can be used to find multiples of the highest number of units in any base up to base ten. For example, multiples of 9 in base ten, of 8 in base nine, of 7 in base eight, and so on.

### Working in base ten

To find the product of $9 \times 7$:

**a** number the fingers from 1 to 10 beginning with the left thumb and ending with the right thumb; and
**b** fold down the finger indicating the multiplier (7). The number of fingers to the left of 7 are counted to find the number of tens in the answer, i.e. 6.

### Multiplication: method 2

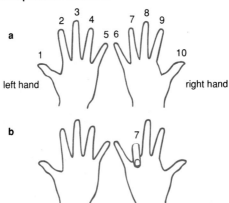

The number of fingers to the right of 7 are counted to find the number of units in the answer, i.e. 3.

Therefore $9 \times 7 = 63$.

**Working in bases of less than ten**

To find the product of $7_8$ (base eight) $\times 4_8$ (base eight):

**c** Only the number of fingers equal to the base are used and all other fingers are folded out of the way. For example, if using base eight, the fingers are numbered from 1 to 8, beginning with the left thumb as before.

**d** The finger indicating the multiplier is folded down (4). The number of fingers to the left and right of number 4 are counted to find the tens and units respectively in the answer. So, $7_8 \times 4_8 = 34_8$.

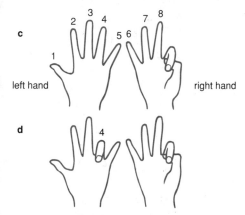

## MAGIC SQUARES

A square with four spaces across and four down is
called a 4-power square.

When numbers are arranged in a 4-power square so that
the numerical total of each line, horizontally, vertically
and diagonally, is the same, the arrangement is known
as a magic square, as shown in the two examples of 4-
power squares.

**Magic square with constant 50**

| 17 | 6  | 20 | 7  |
|----|----|----|----|
| 16 | 11 | 13 | 10 |
| 5  | 18 | 8  | 19 |
| 12 | 15 | 9  | 14 |

**Magic square with constant 58**

| 13 | 8  | 22 | 15 |
|----|----|----|----|
| 18 | 19 | 9  | 12 |
| 7  | 14 | 16 | 21 |
| 20 | 17 | 11 | 10 |

Magic squares can also be of other powers, e.g. this is a
basic 5-power square, with a constant of 65, made
using all the numbers from 1 to 25.

| 17 | 24 | 1  | 8  | 15 |
|----|----|----|----|----|
| 23 | 5  | 7  | 14 | 16 |
| 4  | 6  | 13 | 20 | 22 |
| 10 | 12 | 19 | 21 | 3  |
| 11 | 18 | 25 | 2  | 9  |

**A sample 4-power magic square to complete**
Only numbers from 1 to 16 should be used to fill in the
spaces in the square so that all the rows add up to the
constant 34, horizontally, vertically and diagonally.
Solutions to all the number puzzles are given at the end
of this chapter.

|    | 3  |    | 14 |
|----|----|----|----|
|    |    |    |    |
| 8  |    |    | 12 |
| 11 |    | 6  |    |

**The bonus**

A rich merchant wanted to give his apprentice a bonus for working so well all year, but he also wanted to make the lad use his wits, so he devised a plan.

The merchant placed 1000 coins on the table in front of the apprentice. He told the lad to draw five squares and arrange the coins in piles at the corners of the squares, so that there would be a total of 50 coins in each of the five squares.

In addition, the apprentice had to draw ten rows by joining the corners of the squares. Each row had to contain a total of 50 coins.

The merchant told the lad that when he had done this he could keep as his bonus any unused coins.

This is how the apprentice began to arrange the coins. Can you complete the diagram and find out how many coins the apprentice got as a bonus?

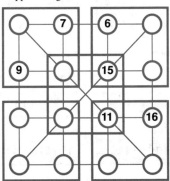

## Four more 4-power magic squares

All these squares not only have horizontals, verticals and diagonals that each total a constant, but the sum of the four numbers in the corners, and the sum of the four numbers in the centre of the square, also result in the same constant.

Complete squares **a** to **d** to produce the constant given for each square.

**a** constant 34, using all the numbers from 1 to 16 inclusive.

| 1 | | | |
|---|---|---|---|
| | 3 | | |
| | | | 2 |
| 14 | | | 11 |

**b** constant 46

| 8 | | 14 | |
|---|---|---|---|
| | 19 | | 5 |
| 11 | | | |
| | | 9 | |

**c** constant 54

| | 21 | | |
|---|---|---|---|
| 12 | | 11 | |
| 19 | | | |
| | 10 | 14 | |

**d** constant 62

| 20 | | | 23 |
|---|---|---|---|
| | | 16 | |
| | | 14 | |
| 10 | 22 | | |

**Some 5-power magic squares**
Complete the following magic squares to make the constants indicated.

**a** constant 65

| 2 | 15 |   |   | 8 |
|----|----|----|----|----|
| 10 |    |    |    |    |
|    |    |    |    |    |
| 14 |    |    | 4  |    |
|    |    | 9  |    |    |

**b** constant 70

|    |    | 26 |    | 3  |
|----|----|----|----|----|
|    |    | 19 |    | 20 |
| 18 |    |    | 6  |    |
|    |    |    |    |    |
|    | 5  |    |    | 21 |

**c** constant 75

|    |    | 7  |    | 9  |
|----|----|----|----|----|
| 10 |    |    |    | 18 |
|    |    |    |    |    |
|    | 14 | 3  |    |    |
|    |    |    |    | 17 |

**d** constant 80

|    | 21 | 10 |    |    |
|----|----|----|----|----|
| 9  |    |    | 26 | 15 |
|    | 8  |    |    |    |
|    |    |    |    |    |
|    | 27 |    |    |    |

**e** design a 5-power square from scratch, with a constant of 85.

|   |   |   |   |   |
|---|---|---|---|---|
|   |   |   |   |   |
|   |   |   |   |   |
|   |   |   |   |   |
|   |   |   |   |   |

## Superior 4-power magic squares

In these squares, in addition to the basic horizontal, vertical and diagonal lines totalling one constant, all the numbers that form squares within the main square also total that constant.

Finally, the number in any corner added to the three numbers diagonally across the opposite corner is also equal to the constant.

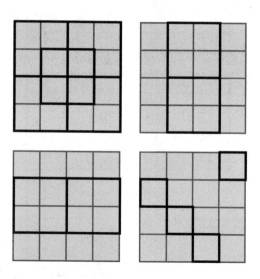

Complete the superior squares **a** and **b** to produce the constants shown.

**a** constant 38

| 5 | | | |
|---|---|---|---|
| | 17 | | 7 |
| | | | |
| | 12 | 9 | |

**b** constant 42

| | | 14 | |
|---|---|---|---|
| | 17 | | |
| | | | 18 |
| | 16 | 9 | |

## SOLUTIONS
### A sample 4-power magic square to complete
The constant is 34. Notice that all the figures from 1 to 16 are used.

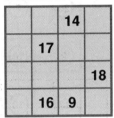

| 2 | 3 | 15 | 14 |
|---|---|---|---|
| 13 | 16 | 4 | 1 |
| 8 | 5 | 9 | 12 |
| 11 | 10 | 6 | 7 |

**The bonus**
The bonus was 800 coins.

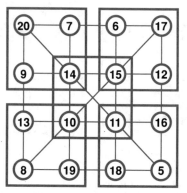

**Four more 4-power magic squares**

**a** constant 34, using all the numbers from 1 to16

| 1  | 15 | 10 | 8  |
|----|----|----|----|
| 12 | 6  | 3  | 13 |
| 7  | 9  | 16 | 2  |
| 14 | 4  | 5  | 11 |

**b** constant 46

| 8  | 7  | 14 | 17 |
|----|----|----|----|
| 12 | 19 | 10 | 5  |
| 11 | 4  | 13 | 18 |
| 15 | 16 | 9  | 6  |

**c** constant 54

| 6 | 21 | 9 | 18 |
|---|----|---|----|
| 12 | 15 | 11 | 16 |
| 19 | 8 | 20 | 7 |
| 17 | 10 | 14 | 13 |

**d** constant 62

| 20 | 8 | 11 | 23 |
|----|---|----|----|
| 15 | 19 | 16 | 12 |
| 17 | 13 | 14 | 18 |
| 10 | 22 | 21 | 9 |

**Some 5-power magic squares**

**a** constant 65

| 2 | 15 | 17 | 23 | 8 |
|---|----|----|----|---|
| 10 | 22 | 1 | 20 | 12 |
| 21 | 19 | 13 | 7 | 5 |
| 14 | 6 | 25 | 4 | 16 |
| 18 | 3 | 9 | 11 | 24 |

**b** constant 70

| 7 | 11 | 26 | 23 | 3 |
|---|----|----|----|---|
| 12 | 19 | 4 | 15 | 20 |
| 18 | 22 | 14 | 6 | 10 |
| 8 | 13 | 24 | 9 | 16 |
| 25 | 5 | 2 | 17 | 21 |

**c** constant 75

| 13 | 24 | 7 | 22 | 9 |
|----|----|---|----|---|
| 10 | 4 | 27 | 16 | 18 |
| 19 | 25 | 15 | 5 | 11 |
| 12 | 14 | 3 | 26 | 20 |
| 21 | 8 | 23 | 6 | 17 |

**d** constant 80

| 19 | 21 | 10 | 5 | 25 |
|----|----|----|---|----|
| 9 | 18 | 12 | 26 | 15 |
| 28 | 8 | 16 | 24 | 4 |
| 17 | 6 | 20 | 14 | 23 |
| 7 | 27 | 22 | 11 | 13 |

**e** constant 85

| 23 | 5  | 8  | 22 | 27 |
|----|----|----|----|----|
| 10 | 28 | 18 | 15 | 14 |
| 25 | 21 | 17 | 13 | 9  |
| 20 | 19 | 16 | 6  | 24 |
| 7  | 12 | 26 | 29 | 11 |

**Superior 4-power magic squares**

**a** constant 38

| 5  | 6  | 11 | 16 |
|----|----|----|----|
| 10 | 17 | 4  | 7  |
| 8  | 3  | 14 | 13 |
| 15 | 12 | 9  | 2  |

**b** constant 42

| 10 | 3  | 14 | 15 |
|----|----|----|----|
| 12 | 17 | 8  | 5  |
| 7  | 6  | 11 | 18 |
| 13 | 16 | 9  | 4  |

# 8. Paper games

## STEPPING THROUGH THE JACK OF HEARTS

A small pair of sharp scissors and the jack of hearts, from a damaged pack of playing cards, will be needed. Any other card may be used, if preferred.

**1** Fold the card in half, lengthways.

**2** Cut a slit along the crease, leaving 5 mm of card uncut at both ends.

**3** At the top of the card, cut across its breadth, from its folded side, to within a few millimetres of its outer edges.

**4** Make the second cut from the outer edge, stopping within a few millimetres of the crease.

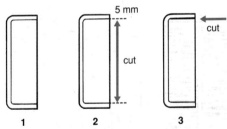

**5** Make similar cuts, alternately, all the way down the card, making the last cut from the folded side.

**6** Unfold the card and lay it flat.

**7** Gently pull the narrow ends apart.

**8** The card becomes a large, thin circle through which a person can step.

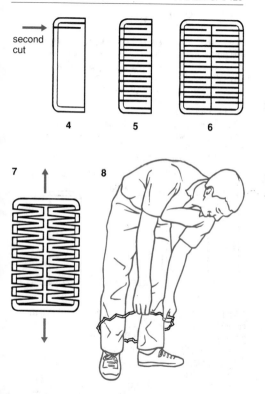

second cut

4

5

6

7

8

## DRAWING CARTOONS

First, the difference between a funny drawing, a
caricature and a cartoon should be understood.

### Funny drawing

A funny drawing is a realistic drawing showing people,
animals, objects, etc., in funny situations or doing
funny things. To make funny pictures, a reasonable
ability to draw and a sense of humour are needed.

**Caricature**

A caricature is an exaggeration of a realistic likeness to reveal, suggest or emphasise foibles, characteristics, attitudes and behaviour.

Caricatures range from the unflattering to the evil and ugly, and are usually drawn of actual people in the public eye: politicians, entertainers, royalty, media stars and sportspeople. Recognisable types of animal, plant or object, such as specific makes of car are also caricatured.

Drawing skills and creative interpretation are vital for successful caricaturing.

**Examples of caricature**

Groucho Marx

Charles de Gaulle

Charlie Chaplin

**Cartoon**

A cartoon is a few simple lines presenting the idea of a type of person or animal.

No advanced drawing skills are necessary. The conventions of drawing cartoons can be learnt by anyone who can hold a pencil. An ability to draw realistically can be a stumbling block for successful cartooning because of a tendency to add too many embellishments.

A sense of humour is essential: the quirkier, the better. An open mind, fascinated with all the facets of humanity, is the breeding ground for great cartoons.

## Some basic conventions of cartoon drawing

Simplicity, expression and movement are combined to
create an illusion. The best drawing tool is a fine felt-
or fibre-tipped pen which gives a good black line. Also,
these types of pen tend to be easier to manage than
biros, which give finer, more wiry lines.

It is a good idea to begin with faces. A face is drawn in
the following way:

1 the nose, a hooked line facing left or right;
2 the eyes, two small scribbled dots on the nose;
3 the mouth, a slightly wobbly line;

4 then the face shape, hair and an ear;
5 finally, eyebrows are added, if they will make the
basic expression more friendly, miserable, puzzled, etc.

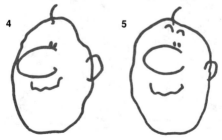

## Style

While every line in a cartoon is carefully thought out
and contrived to give an illusion, it is actually drawn
quickly to communicate a sense of spontaneity. Practice
is the only way to achieve this.

Drawing 40 or 50 faces with each type of expression, at
speed, will help to develop an unmistakable personal
style. This is how professional cartoonists make it
appear so easy! Every cartoon they make may have
been the result of 20 or more attempts.

## Selecting the final cartoon

Among faces drawn repeatedly on a sheet of paper,
there will be only one or two that exactly communicate
the desired expression. These can be signed, cut out and
stuck on paper to keep or to use in a larger cartoon.

**Cartoon signatures**

Every newspaper has its regular cartoonists,
recognisable by their style, the cartoon characters they
have created and by their signature.

All cartoons should be signed. It is worth taking a little
time to develop a personal signature.

## Some cartoons of male faces by Pilkie

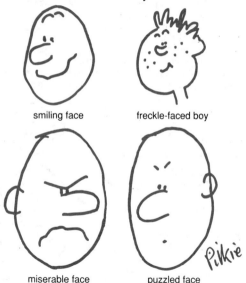

smiling face            freckle-faced boy

miserable face          puzzled face

## Adding features

Remember to draw the nose and the eyes first. The
mouth and the face can then be added in different
shapes and sizes. Necks too can be added, as in the
examples shown overleaf.

**1** The face can be drawn in two parts, one curve for the
chin and the other with a squiggle to indicate a bald
head with some hair at the back.

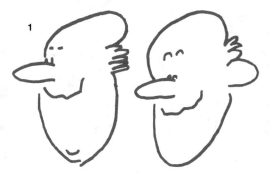

**2** Many bald men wear a moustache, shown by a
squiggle under the nose before the chin is drawn.
Stubble can be added using dots.

**3** A whole head of hair is a bigger squiggle over the top
of the head, finished with a large hook-shaped line for
the ear.

**4** Curly lines, sharp zig-zags, scribbles and long wavy
lines all indicate different hair styles.

**5** Moustaches and beards obliterate the mouth, but can be turned up or down to give expression, which is enhanced by the eyebrows.

**6** A wobbly V-shaped line turns a smile into a laugh and a scribble in the corner of the V makes a "noisy" laugh.

When filling in a space, always leave bits of white paper showing through. This adds life. A completely filled-in area is deadening.

**7** Eyes often get narrower when laughing, so they should be drawn as a short dash.

**8** A "horsey" laugh needs a set of teeth.

**9** Spectacles come in all shapes and sizes. The lenses are usually drawn first, with the nose, and the arms of the glasses added later to suit the hair style and ears. Eyes can be moved around within the lenses.

### Drawing cartoons of women

The order of drawing is still the same as for the basic male face, but with a smaller nose and mouth.

**1** The cartoon convention to indicate a female mouth is to place a dot across the line of the mouth.

**2** Hairstyles can be indicated with a wide variety of creative scribbles. Observing how people wear their hair, and translating the style with a simple scribble, is the essence of successful cartooning.

**3** Earrings and other adornments should be indicated with simple lines. Too much detail ruins cartoons.

**Drawing cartoon kids**

Children's faces are drawn in the same order as before,
with three special features: a small, turned-up nose; the
mouth is placed lower in the face than for cartoons of
adults; and a very thin neck.

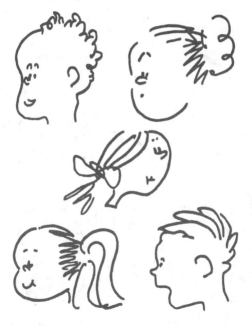

**Baby cartoons**

Babies are even more difficult to draw than children.
With virtually no hair, it is vital that the head and face
shapes give the right illusion. An upside-down violin or
a broad bean are the easiest ways to describe the correct
shape.

Freckles or a single strand of unruly hair add
authenticity. Crying babies have enormous mouths.

**Whole bodies**

Bodies are usually quite out of proportion to the head and are often on the move.

A knowledge of anatomy is not necessary, as clothes cover most cartoon bodies, and only a suggestion of body shape is necessary. Hands only have three fingers: fourth fingers are unnecessary details.

The conventionally suited man can be drawn in stages:

**1** head and neck;
**2** V-shaped collar and tie;
**3** jacket lapels;
**4** jacket with arms and hands;
**5** trousers with shoes (everyone develops their own drawing style for footwear).

A shadow fixes him to the ground.

## Action

Cartoons are always active. Even when cartoon figures are asleep, movement is shown by snores and buzzes. Placing a shadow a little below the feet gives a sense of action.

Simple curves or lines illustrating movement add activity, while a few drops of sweat can convey a great deal about energy and mood.

Thoughts are usually placed in a cloud-bubble.

Comments are printed within a speech-arrow.

**Examples of active cartoons**

## Objects and animals

**1** Hats can be drawn using two basic shapes.
**a** The crown is drawn as a semicircle or arc, which can be increased in length or breadth, as desired.
**b** The brim is drawn as a teardrop lying on its side. Adjustments are made to these shapes with the addition of faces, flowers, fruit, etc.
**2** Umbrellas and sticks, bags and briefcases, are kept simple.
**3** Some things that are hard to draw can be suggested: for example, lines of movement obscuring a bicycle and the back of a bus are enough to convey the relevant messages.

### Examples of cartoon objects

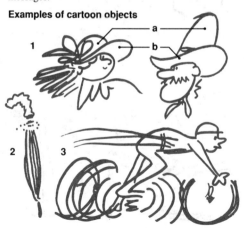

Animals are extremely difficult to draw as cartoons unless their anatomy is studied carefully.
When in doubt, silhouettes can be useful or animals can be hidden behind hedges, with just a head showing to suggest a horse or a cow.

**Examples of cartoon animals**

**Animating objects**

If drawing cartoon people defeats you, objects, such as
milk bottles, can be animated to convey a message.

Objects are useful, too, when making cartoon puns. For
example:
**1** wringing wet;
**2** tomato sauce;

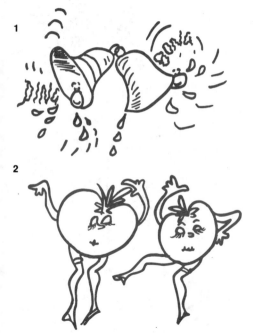

**3** telly addicts; and
**4** Peking duck.

Try to draw cartoons with the following captions:
snap dragons; fountain pen; soap opera; minimum;
spring onions; and then think of some original puns.
Studying cartoons drawn by professionals teaches much
about cartooning, but the development of a personal
style is essential for success.

# 9. Action games

Games that depend on the skilful use of the hands can
be very satisfying. Shadow play is something the
imaginative player can develop into a fine art, while
juggling requires good coordination and an awareness
of three-dimensional space.

There are also many games for two or more people that
can be practised alone to advantage, such as domino
patience, fivestones and jacks.

## DOMINO PATIENCE

This is an excellent way of learning to make the best
choices in any game of dominoes. A complete set of
dominoes should be shuffled, face down, on the table.
This is called the "boneyard".

**1** From the boneyard take five dominoes, turn them
face up and select one to place in the centre from which
to build.

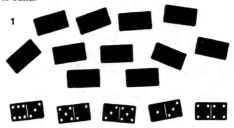

**2** Add as many of the remaining four as possible, to
either end of the domino in the centre, to form a chain.

**2**

**3** Take more dominoes from the boneyard to replace the ones used, i.e. making the number up to five again.

**3**

**4** Continue to build on either end of the chain, aiming to use up all the dominoes.

**4**

### Variations

**1** The game can be made easier by using a hand of six or seven dominoes.

**2** Instead of making a random chain, conditions can be introduced, such as ensuring that the joining ends add up to seven or eight.

**3** It is interesting to turn the whole boneyard face up and to play against the clock.

# FIVESTONES

This is an old game, played internationally under
different names such as knucklebones and chuckies.

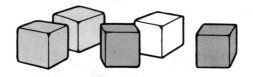

Fivestones can be bought as five ceramic or plastic
cubes with rounded corners and of different colours.
Small pebbles or old dice make good substitutes.

## Aim

The aim is to successfully complete a series of short
games. With two players, the games are played in an
agreed order, and the first to complete all of them wins.
Solo players can practise each game and then the whole
sequence, keeping a record of successes to compare
with the next attempt, aiming to improve on previous
scores.

## Rules

Beginners can play according to the basic rules, more
advanced players should aim to keep to the strict rules.
The basic rules allow the player to make several
attempts at each game, and to touch or move stones
other than the ones intended.

The strict rules allow only one attempt at each game in
the sequence and touching stones, other than the ones in
play, disqualifies the player.

### Ones

All the fivestones are thrown upwards from the palm
and caught on the back of the hand; they are then
thrown up from the back of the hand and caught in the
palm. If all five are caught, the player goes on to the
next game.

If more than one is caught, one is retained and the rest
are put into the other hand.

The fallen stones are then picked up, one at a time, as
the retained stone is thrown into the air by the same
hand.

Strict rules: one stone must be picked up during each
throw.

**Twos**

The five stones are scattered onto the table. One stone is picked up and thrown into the air as two are picked up from the table and transferred to the other hand. One stone is thrown into the air as the remaining two stones are picked up.

Basic rules: the stones on the table may be nudged closer together as one stone is thrown from the hand into the air.

Strict rules: the stones must be picked up from wherever they are scattered.

**Threes**

Played as twos, one stone being picked up and then three, or three and then one.

**Fours**

Played as twos, but all four stones must be picked up during one throw.

**Pecks**

This game is played as for ones, but the stones must be retained in the throwing hand and not transferred to the other hand.

## Bushels

The aim is first to throw all five stones upwards together (**1**), catch them on the back of the hand (**2**), then throw them up again and catch them in the palm (**3**). If not all five stones are caught, the player continues by throwing the remaining stones up from the hand (**4**), while picking up the fallen stones one at a time (**5**). The thrown stones must be caught in the same hand that picks up the fallen stones (**6**).

**Bushels**

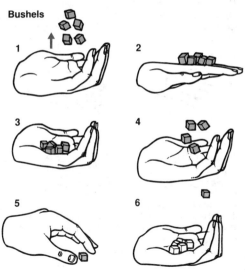

## Claws

If all five stones are thrown and caught on the back of
the hand, they can be thrown again and caught in the
palm.

If either move fails, the game continues by retaining
any caught stones on the back of the hand and picking
up the remaining stones between the fingers or the
thumb and forefinger, with only one stone between any
two fingers or between finger and thumb (**1**).

The stones on the back of the hand are then thrown
(**2**) and caught in the palm (**3**), and the stones between
the fingers are worked into the palm without being
dropped (**4**).

**Claws**

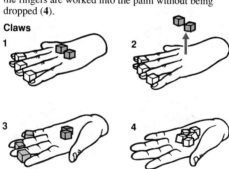

## Ones under the arch

The stones are scattered. One is picked up, to throw,
and an arch is made with the forefinger and thumb of
the other hand (**1**).

As the stone is thrown upwards, one stone is knocked
under the arch (**2**). The thrown stone is caught in the

palm of the throwing hand (**3**).
This is repeated until all four stones have been knocked
under the arch.
The arch is then removed. As the stone is thrown
upwards, all four stones must then be picked up at
once, from wherever they went as they were knocked
under the arch.

### Ones under the arch

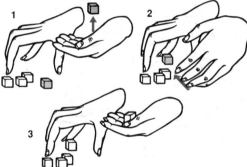

### Twos under the arch
This game is played as before, but the stones must be
knocked under the arch in pairs.

### Threes under the arch
Played as before, but the stones are knocked under the
arch as one and then three, or three and then one.

### Fours under the arch
Played as before, but all four stones must be knocked
under the arch during one throw.

## Stables

This series of games is played in the same way as the Arches series, except that, instead of arches, the inactive hand forms four "stables" by spreading the fingers. No more than one stone may be knocked into each stable.

**Stables**

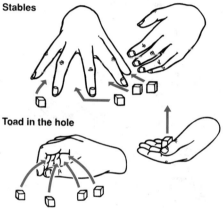

**Toad in the hole**

## Toad in the hole

This series is played as those before but the hand makes a cave-like shape into which to flip or drop the stones.

## Sweep the floor

This series is played as before, but each part consists of several moves, each done with a statement, after the initial scattering of the stones.

**1a** As the stone is thrown, the throwing hand strokes the table and the player says: "sweep the floor".

**b** As the stone is thrown, the throwing hand moves another stone to a new position: "move the chair".
**c** As the stone is thrown, the "chair" stone is picked up and held in the throwing hand: "pick it up".
**d** As the stone is thrown, the "chair" is then put down again: "put it there".
**2** Actions **a** to **d** are repeated, but this time they are done twice during each throw.
**3** Actions **a** to **d** are performed three times during each throw.
**4** Actions **a** to **d** are done four times during each throw and, once these and all the previous moves have been successfully completed, all four stones should be picked up during one throw.

**Sweep the floor**

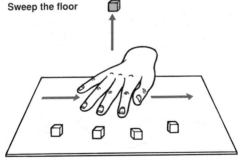

**Backward ones, twos, threes and fours**
This series of games is played as Ones, Twos, Threes and Fours, except that the stones are caught first on the back of the hand and then on the palm.

### Snake in the grass

Four stones are placed, several centimetres apart, in a
row. As the fifth stone is thrown, the leading stone is
moved in and out around the other three until it arrives
back at its original position, as shown in the diagram.
As many throws as desired are allowed, but the aim is
to use a minimum.

### Snake in the grass

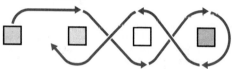

### Square sweep

Four stones are placed at the corners of a square, about
30 cm (12 in) apart. The aim is to pick up all four at
once during one throw of the remaining stone.

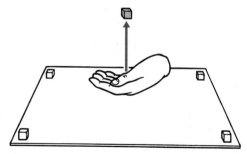

### Big Ben

A tower is built using four of the stones. During each throw of the remaining stone, one stone is removed from the tower and placed in the other hand. As the last stone is removed, the thrown stone should also be caught in the other hand, so that the game finishes with all five stones in the non-throwing hand.

**Big Ben**

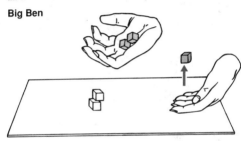

### The Tower of London

This game is Big Ben played in reverse. Four stones are held in the non-throwing hand. As the fifth stone is thrown upwards, the throwing hand takes a stone and places it on the table.

During the next throw, another stone is placed on top of the first, and so on until all four are built into a tower.

### More fivestones games

Other games can be invented as the player becomes more and more skilled. The sequence of games can be decided in advance, and the skilled solo player may also like to use time limits.

## JACKS

These games are very similar to fivestones except that
jacks is played with five jacks and a small rubber ball,
about 2.5 cm (1 in) across. Sets of jacks can be bought
which have a three-dimensional arrangement of three
bars with small balls on each end. Jacks can also be
played with a set of fivestones, or five small pebbles,
and a rubber ball.

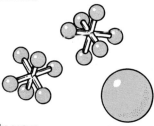

### The jacks games

All the fivestone games, except the building games, are
played with jacks, with one fundamental difference.
Only the ball is thrown, so there are five jacks, or
stones, to pick up or move, instead of four, and at each
throw the ball is allowed to bounce once before being
caught.

## JUGGLING

To learn the basics of juggling, three beanbags are
needed. A cube of fabric filled with dried beans and
firmly sewed together makes a good beanbag.
A fabric cube of between 5 and 8 cm³ (2 and 3 in³) is
about the right size for an adult. Size should be adjusted
to fit the hand.

The bag should fit comfortably in the centre of the hand
and feel malleable, but not so loose that the fabric
follows the beans when thrown.
The beanbag should not be held in the fingers. For
successful juggling, the whole hand is used.

### How to begin
The juggler should stand in a relaxed way, with a
beanbag in one hand. Elbows should be fairly close to
the body and the hands held at waist height.

**How to begin**

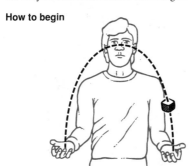

The bag is thrown in an arc that is as wide as the body, with its peak at eye level.

The aim is to practise throwing the bag easily and consistently, back and forth, over this arc without putting any spin on it.

**Exchanging two bags**

Standing as before, a bag is held in the centre of each hand.

**1** One bag is thrown upwards.

**2** As it reaches eye level, the second bag is thrown so that the two bags pass each other below the top of the arc, at about 15 cm (6 in) above the hand.

**3** The first bag is caught as the second begins to drop into the other hand.

The bags should follow arcs in the same vertical plane as each other, the first making a larger arc than the second.

**3**

### The juggle

**1** Basic juggling is done with three bags.

**1**

**2** Beginning with the hand holding two bags, a bag is thrown through an arc, as before.

**2**

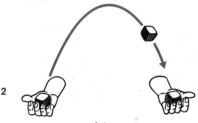

**3** A second bag from the other hand is thrown in a smaller arc, as before.

**4** The third bag is thrown as the first bag lands in the hand.

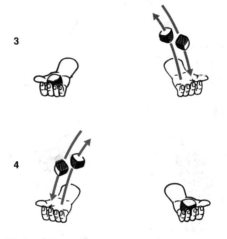

The juggle is continued with a bag being thrown each time a flying bag is dropping from the peak of its arc. In this way, only one bag is actually flying at a time but it will appear as though three bags are on the move. When the basic juggle has been achieved, more bags can be added and a greater variety of styles of catching can be introduced.

## SHADOW FIGURES

The hands, when placed between a source of bright light and a plain wall, will cast a shadow. When making shadows, it is easier to control what is happening by watching the shadow and not the hands.

light source

The shadow becomes clearer and sharper if the hands are moved closer to the wall, and it can be softened by moving them closer to the light source.

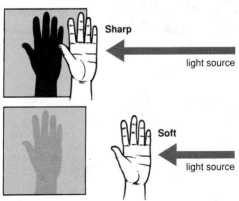

**Sharp**

light source

**Soft**

light source

An outstretched hand held parallel to the wall will cast a similar shadow. When the hand is turned at an angle to the wall, however, the shape of the shadow changes.

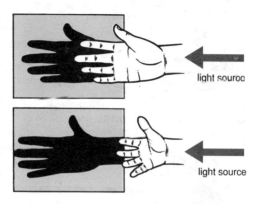

light source

light source

By bending the fingers and using both hands, some easily recognisable animal shapes can be made. When the fingers are moved, the duck can be made to quack, the dog to bark and the bird to fly.

When these basic shapes have been achieved, more complex shadows can be attempted and made to move. For example, the rabbit's ears can flap, its forelegs can tap on the ground and, with a little care, it can be made to sit upright by turning the hands upwards.

**Examples of hand-shadow animals**

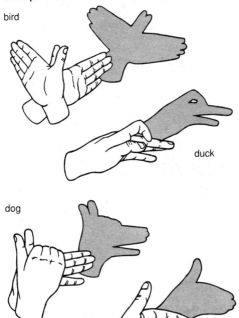

bird

duck

dog

sheep

**Examples of
hand-shadow
animals**
(continued)

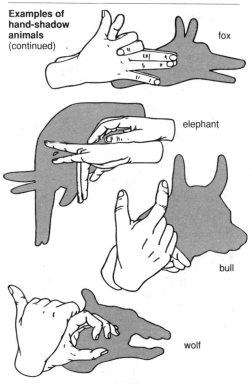

fox

elephant

bull

wolf

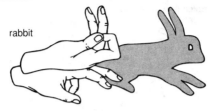

rabbit

Human faces are more difficult to make, unless rather craggy faces are selected, as shown in these examples.

**Examples of hand-shadow faces**

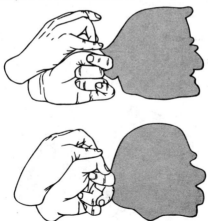

**Examples of hand-shadow faces**
(continued)

More complicated shadows can be made using small
props, such as collars or hats, cut from odd pieces of
card.

**Bearded man with a hat**

The hat shape is cut from cardboard and held between
the hands. When cutting shapes for props, an extra
piece of cardboard should be allowed for holding the
object. It is worth experimenting to get the right size to
fit the hands.

### Rowing a boat

Cardboard shapes for the hat, an oar and a boat are
required for this figure. The hat is held between the first
and second fingers and the oar is attached to the thumb
with sticky tape, so that it can be moved as if rowing.

### Gone fishing

The same figure in a boat can do some very convincing
fishing. The rod may have to be a short stick or knitting

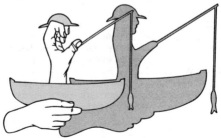

needle with string and a fish-shaped piece of card
attached. The rod should be strapped firmly to the
thumb. By using a small hook to which diverse shapes
can be attached, it becomes possible for the "angler" to
pull a variety of fish and other objects out of the water.

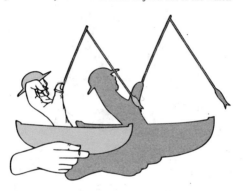

### Table tennis
A hat and the shape of a table tennis bat, cut out of
cardboard, are needed for this figure. The bat should
have a long enough handle so that it can be taped to the
thumb. When the thumb is moved, the figure will
appear to be hitting a ball. The figure can play other
games using other equipment, such as a "tennis raquet".
A real challenge would be to make a figure playing
snooker.

### Out for the night

The shape of a top hat, cut from cardboard, a real scarf
and a small bottle are the props needed for this figure.
The hat is held between the thumb and forefinger. With
practice, the figure can be made to tip his head
backwards and drink from the bottle.

**Domestic battle**

It takes considerable skill to work the hands to make two figures that are having an argument. Each will need a hat, held between the fingers, and a stick, umbrella or broom shape which should be taped to the thumbs.

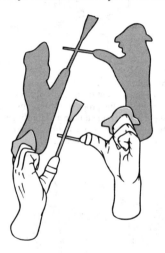

# Index